BIBLE HISTORY IN OUTLINE

GENESIS — ESTHER

by

Roy Clark Maddux

BAKER BOOK HOUSE
Grand Rapids, Michigan

Copyright, 1972, by
Roy Clark Maddux

Baker Book House ISBN:0-8010-5895-3

PHOTOLITHOPRINTED BY CUSHING - MALLOY, INC.
ANN ARBOR, MICHIGAN, UNITED STATES OF AMERICA
1972

To

The Administration and Faculty of Southern Baptist College
College City, Walnut Ridge, Arkansas

FOREWORD

These outlines are based on the King James version of the Bible. Other versions have been used for comparison and clarity. The temptation to use modern parlance won in word choices at times, but the meanings will give little trouble to the modern reader.

It is the hope of the author that these outlines will prove helpful to the busy Bible student as have the previous three books of Bible outlines, THE PSALMS IN OUTLINE; OUTLINE STUDIES IN JOB, PROVERBS, ECCLESIASTES, AND SONG OF SONGS; and THE PROPHETS IN OUTLINE, published by Baker Book House, Grand Rapids, Michigan.

R. C. M.

GENESIS

CHAPTER 1
I. Creation's week.
   A. Prelude to declaration.
      1. Primal outline.
      2. Intangible form.
      3. Absence of light.
      4. Motion in Spirit.
   B. First imperative.
      1. No restraints permitted.
      2. Unreserved compliance.
   C. Divine inspection.
      1. Acceptance announced.
      2. Adequate division.
      3. Appropriately named divisions.
      4. Accurate time designation.
   D. Division by firmament.
      1. Atmospheric from fluid.
      2. Firmament named.
      3. Time period.
   E. Division below firmament.
      1. Land from liquid.
      2. Designated divisions.
      3. Earth's mission begins.
         a. Flora classes.
         b. Self propagation.
      4. Time period.
   F. Division in firmament.
      1. Designated spheres.
      2. Designated purposes.
      3. Division in labor.
      4. Time period.
   G. Water's mission authorized.
      1. Fauna's beginning.
         a. Fish, fowl, reptile
         b. Self-propagation.
      2. Divine blessing.
      3. Divine commission.
      4. Time period.
   H. Earth's mission continues.
      1. Land fauna.
      2. Distinct division.
      3. Self-propagation.
      4. Creator's approval.
      5. Special creation.
         a. Distinct *familia*.
         b. Distinct design.
         c. Distinct dominion.
      6. Divine approval and blessing.
      7. Creation's safeguards.
      8. Creator's acclaim.
      9. Time period.

CHAPTER 2
      10. Period of rest.
II. Creation's formation.
   A. Plan in Mind of God.
   B. Provision for growth.
   C. Provender, but no tiller.
   D. The earth, mother of all.
   E. The planted garden.
   F. Man's dominion.
   G. Man's provision.
   H. Man's prohibition.

I. Man's nominal mission.
　　J. Man's loneliness.
III. Creation's completion.
　　A. Man, the source of humanity.
　　B. Woman from man.
　　　　1. Recognized.
　　　　2. Named.
　　　　3. Accepted.
　　C. Innocent purity.

CHAPTER 3

I. Subtle suspicion.
　　A. Question for doubt.
　　B. False interpretation.
　　C. Shortcut to humanity's aspirations.
　　D. Shortsighted dubious achievement.
　　E. Futile protection for guilt.
　　　　1. Hid nakedness.
　　　　2. Hid presence.
II. Self-examination divinely inspired.
　　A. Where?
　　B. Who?
　　C. What?
　　D. Buck-passing.
　　　　1. Man blames God.
　　　　2. Woman blames man (implied).
III. Equitable judgment.
　　A. Serpent condemned to low estate.
　　B. Promised Redeemer.
　　C. Woman's lot decreed.
　　D. Man's life of labor.
　　E. Man's physical destiny.
　　F. Humanity's mother.
　　G. Vicarious remission.
　　H. Man's further prohibition.
　　I. Tree of Life protected.

CHAPTER 4

I. The beginning of parenthood.
　　A. God honoring.
　　B. Manifold.
II. Division of labor.
　　A. Agronomy.
　　B. Animal husbandry.
III. Division of worship.
　　A. Selfish convenience.
　　B. Vicarious atonement.
IV. Diverse interpretation.
　　A. Peevish, short-sighted view.
　　B. Heart-probing examination.
　　C. Selfish enthronement.
　　D. Human solution.
　　　　1. Word power tried.
　　　　2. Life devaluated.
　　E. Brotherhood challenged.
　　F. Sin's chastisement.
　　　　1. Earth's rejection.
　　　　2. Society's exclusion.
　　G. Sinner's complaint.
　　　　1. Ponderous price.
　　　　2. Fearful fugitive.
　　H. Sin's harvest.
　　　　1. Division of occupations.
　　　　2. Polygamy.
　　　　3. Like father, like son.
V. Parenthood's condolence.
　　A. God's place in life.
　　B. Man's relationship with God.

CHAPTER 5

I. Man's progenitors.
　　A. God the Creator in likeness.
　　B. God the Designator of sex.
　　C. God the Blesser.
　　D. God the Namer.

GENESIS

II. Man's progeny.
  A. Father to representative son.
  B. Total life span for Creator's purpose.
  C. Varied life expectancy.
  D. Ideal walk of one man.
    1. Lived for God
    2. Communed with God.
    3. Lives with God.
  E. *Patre* prophetic.
    1. Hopes in a son.
    2. Hopes for curse's recall.
    3. Ten generations from Adam

CHAPTER 6

I. Natural procreation.
  A. Population "explosion."
  B. Outward attractiveness.
  C. Subjective choice.
  D. Emphasis in the physical (vv. 2, 5).
II. Spiritual evaluation.
  A. Two ways contrasted.
  B. Spiritual education.
  C. The bounds of time.
  D. Natural man's direction.
  E. God's measure.
  F. God's judgment.
  G. Nature without God.
III. Spiritual procreation.
  A. God's choice.
  B. Noah's choice.
    1. In worship.
    2. In walk.
    3. In family well-being.
  C. Separated lives.
  D. Separated ends.
  E. Full directions.
  F. Full commitment.

CHAPTER 7

I. Command for action.
  A. Commitment compassing.
  B. Complete judgment.
  C. Concern for sustenance.
  D. Compliance time.
    1. Preparation interval.
    2. Prevailing period.
II. Action fitted to command.
  A. Complete obedience.
  B. Maturity established.
  C. Pattern of obedience.
  D. Natural compliance.
III. Destructive action.
  A. Unnatural phenomenon.
  B. Source of water adequate.
  C. More than floating experience.
  D. No refuge in mountains.
  E. Total destruction for air breathers.
IV. The Ark of Safety.
  A. God's command.
  B. God's measures.
  C. God's purpose.

CHAPTER 8

I. God remembers.
  A. First judgment ended.
    1. Deluge stopped.
    2. Deluge decreased.
  B. Terra firma reappears.
  C. Tested for assurance.
II. God re-directs.
  A. Creative purpose in force.
  B. Life principle continued.
  C. Worship prescience reappeared.
III. God reassures.
  A. Sincere adoration accepted.
  B. Judgment method

     C. Individual responsibility asserted.
     D. Life and earth in duo-role.

CHAPTER 9
  I. Man's status.
     A. Control for use.
     B. Use for purpose.
     C. Purpose for judgment.
 II. Man's covenant.
     A. All-inclusive.
     B. Fears for flood fulminated.
     C. The bow of promise.
        1. Natural phenomena.
        2. Duo-viewed.
        3. Far-reaching application.
III. Man's fulfillments.
     A. Work at hand.
     B. Lost power of inhibitions.
     C. Inhumanity to man.
        1. Butt of joke.
        2. Subject of gossip.
     D. Filial respect possible.
     E. Patriarchal usurpation.
     F. Death awaits.

CHAPTER 10
  I. Gentile generations.
     A. Japheth's descendants.
     B. Division of lands.
        1. By tongues.
        2. By families.
        3. By nations.
 II. Canaanite generations.
     A. Ham, the father.
     B. Nimrod, the predator.
     C. Egoists.
     D. Builders of cities.
     E. Prolific people.
     F. Opponents of Israel.
     G. Inner-related but divided.

III. Hebrew generations.
     A. Father of Eber, Shem.
     B. Widespread descendants.
 IV. The Earth's generations.
     A. Division of nations.
     B. After the deluge.

CHAPTER 11
  I. Primal unity.
     A. In migration.
     B. In location.
     C. In projection.
     D. In work.
 II. Divine evaluation.
     A. Plans sans paternity.
     B. Speech sans understanding.
     C. Frustration in confusion.
     D. Significance of Babel.
III. Specific from general.
     A. Review of Shem's progeny.
     B. Background in Ur.
     C. Patriarchal leadership.
     D. Family background.

CHAPTER 12
  I. The call for separation.
     A. No hasty decision.
     B. Complete separation.
     C. Replacements.
 II. The promise in separation.
     A. National greatness.
     B. Personal blessings.
     C. Family recognition.
     D. Reciprocal outreach.
        1. Two-way blessings.
        2. Protection from curses.
        3. World missions.
III. The practice of separation.
     A. Full obedience.
     B. No targets for return.

GENESIS

    C. Objective goals.
- IV. Worship in separation.
  - A. No deterrents in locations.
  - B. Altars in camps.
  - C. Answer to worship.
- V. Direction in separation.
  - A. No turning back.
  - B. No pause for regrets.
  - C. Goal ahead.
- VI. Beyond separation.
  - A. Fear, not trust.
  - B. Breadbasket appeal.
  - C. Personal safety supercedes.
  - D. Divine intervention.
  - E. Wordly rejection.

CHAPTER 13

- I. The wanderer's return.
  - A. To point of departure.
  - B. Material blessings.
  - C. Return in worship.
- II. Magnanimity.
  - A. Selfish strife.
  - B. Choice selflessly granted.
  - C. Narrow vision.
- III. Contrast in prospects.
  - A. Man-made cities.
  - B. Preoccupied possessions.
  - C. The way of sin.
  - D. The way of promise.
  - E. Endless perspective.
  - F. Time and place for worship.

CHAPTER 14

- I. Selfish aggression.
  - A. Kings in power.
  - B. Kings in tribute.
  - C. Kings in rebellion.
  - D. Kings in retribution.
  - E. Kings in defeat.
- II. Selfless Aid.
  - A. The alarm.
  - B. The conclave.
  - C. The strategy.
  - D. The victory.
  - E. The spoils.
- III. Sincere worship.
  - A. The king of Salem (peace)
  - B. The blessings.
  - C. The first tithe.
  - D. The recognition of Deity.
  - E. The shared honor.

CHAPTER 15

- I. The Covenant iterated.
  - A. The Word of Power.
  - B. The limited foresight of man.
  - C. The plan of God.
- II. The past blessings iterated.
  - A. The limited faith of man.
  - B. Faith tested.
  - C. Faith in action.
- III. Vicarious sacrifices.
  - A. The night vision.
  - B. Projected history.
  - C. The remembered covenant.
  - D. The established covenant.

CHAPTER 16

- I. Man's impatience.
  - A. God's answer hurried.
  - B. Vicarious motherhood.
  - C. Selfish glory.
- II. Man's solution.
  - A. Buck-passing not sufficient.
  - B. Loveless corrective measures.
  - C. Loveless sacrifice.

III. God's use of man's blunders.
   A. Promise of progeny.
   B. Self-appraisal for human decisions.
   C. Fulfillment as promised.

CHAPTER 17

I. Covenant renewal.
   A. Authority established.
   B. Walk with words required.
   C. Promised progeny restated.
   D. Name changing (vv. 5, 15).
II. Covenant provisions.
   A. Projected progeny.
   B. Royal progeny.
   C. Permanent quality.
   D. Landed possessions.
   E. Compliance demanded.
III. Covenant proof.
   A. Circumcision established.
   B. Inclusive coverage.
   C. Separation from flesh.
IV. Covenant reactions.
   A. Physical doubt.
   B. Man's limit of God.
   C. God's time limitless.
V. Covenant compliance.
   A. Example of patriarch.
   B. Prompt obedience.
   C. No exceptions.

CHAPTER 18

I. Desert hospitality.
   A. Guests noticed.
   B. Guests invited.
   C. Guests entertained.
II. Deity manifested.
   A. Concern for covenant.
   B. Promises renewed.
   C. Unbelief discerned.
III. Humans reacting.
   A. Doubt.
   B. Limited God.
   C. Face-saving denial.
IV. Missions concern.
   A. Abraham's integrity.
   B. Abraham's dependability.
   C. Abraham's limited prayer.
   D. God's compassion.

CHAPTER 19

I. Family hospitality.
   A. Lot's acceptability.
      1. Elders' place at city gate.
      2. Pressing invitation.
      3. Guests protected.
   B. Lot's commission.
II. Family disloyalty.
   A. Earthly father's empty testimony.
   B. Heavenly Father's insistence.
   C. Place of safety declined.
   D. Command disobeyed.
III. Family perpetuity.
   A. Remembered covenant.
   B. First place of safety deserted.
   C. Hopeless youth.
   D. Youthful selfish solutions.

CHAPTER 20

I. Fear on the throne.
   A. Famine motivation.
   B. Selfish deception.
   C. Innocent heathenism.
II. Fear augmented.
   A. Dream warning.
   B. Heathen reprimand.
   C. Half-truth defense.
III. Fear reproved.

GENESIS

   A. Unmerited gifts.
   B. Enlarged occupational privileges.
   C. The cost of sin.
      1. Sociological outreach.
      2. Progeny limit.
      3. Selfless petition.

CHAPTER 21

I. The visit of Deity.
   A. In performance.
   B. Fulfilled promise.
   C. The name to remember.
II. The verification of agreements.
   A. Rites in solemnity.
   B. Human wonderment.
   C. Response to blessings.
III. The vagaries of domesticity.
   A. Selfish reactions.
      1. Sneers of a son.
      2. Scorn of vicarious motherhood.
      3. Scared fatherhood.
IV. The vision of promise.
   A. Progeny continuation.
   B. Provisions for immediate needs.
   C. Prostrations in distress.
   D. Protection provided.
V. The value of friendship.
   A. Mutual pledges.
   B. Recall of unfriendly actions.
   C. Pledged ownership.
   D. Recognized rights.
   E. Remembrance more than nominal.

CHAPTER 22

I. The test of faith.
   A. The voice of command.
   B. The ear of obedience.
   C. The preparation of compliance.
II. The test of time and place
   A. No snap judgment.
   B. Expressed assurance.
   C. No unanswered questions (vv. 5, 8).
III. The test of action.
   A. Worshipful preparation.
   B. No wishful thinking.
   C. No reservations.
   D. The recognition of faith.
   E. Testimony in name.
IV. The reward of faithfulness.
   A. Full obedience commended.
   B. Endless blessings.
   C. Verification of directive.
   D. Family ties forecast.

CHAPTER 23

I. Death in the family.
   A. Life span.
   B. Geographic space.
   C. Grief's scope.
II. Burial by the family
   A. Burial site sought.
   B. Oriental bargaining.
      1. Cognizance of integrity.
      2. Gift offer.
      3. Purchase offer.
   C. Confirmation in courtesy.
   D. Legal finality.
   E. Completion.

CHAPTER 24

I. Paternal concern.
   A. Son's welfare at heart.
   B. Trusted emissary.
   C. More than word of mouth.
   D. Important mission.

- E. Limitations to demands.
- F. Faith in Divine leadership.

II. Dependable servant.
- A. No procrastination.
- B. Belief in power of prayer.
- C. A "Gideon" test.

III. Dependable fulfillments.
- A. Immediate answer complete.
- B. No limitations.
- C. Presents in confirmation.
- D. Invitation to guest.

IV. Deep concern.
- A. Full background report.
- B. Fulfillment prospects.
- C. Acceptable gifts.
- D. No delay permitted.
- E. Damsel's decision.
- F. Return undertaken.

V. Mission accomplished.
- A. Land of Promise reached.
- B. Mutual concern.
- C. Maidenly modesty.
- D. Full report.
- E. Gracious acceptance.

CHAPTER 25

I. Bloodlines intended.
- A. Second wife.
- B. Second family.
- C. Division of property.
- D. Ground work for conflicts.

II. Two sons in only unity.
- A. Burial site reused.
- B. Israel's tie with Egypt.
  1. Hagar the Egyptian.
  2. Ishmael the son of Abram.
  3. Twelve sons of Ishmael.
  4. Land occupied.

III. Isaac's generation.
- A. Abraham's heir.
- B. Abraham's worship pattern.
- C. Posterity's protagonism.
- D. Differentiations.
  1. Supplanter recognized.
     a. At birth.
     b. In name.
     c. By activities.
  2. Supplanter's first victory.

CHAPTER 26

I. Famine migration.
- A. Limited in scope.
- B. Heir to promise.
- C. Heir to covenant.

II. Faith of narrow vision.
- A. Selfish subterfuge.
- B. Subtle snooping.
- C. Stern scolding.

III. Fulfilled material blessings.
- A. Fields respond.
- B. Flocks replenished.
- C. Fulmination reverberating
  1. Jealousy.
  2. False claims.
  3. Aggressible possesssion.

IV. Friendship pledges.
- A. Reiterated promises.
- B. Follows worship.
- C. Wells free from strife.
- D. Feast of friendship.

V. Family frustrations.
- A. Wandering fancies.
- B. Unsanctioned marriages.

CHAPTER 27

I. Patriarchal concern.
- A. Limited vision.
- B. Life uncertainty.

- C. Living appetites.
- D. Lasting last blessing.
II. Matriarchal intrigue.
- A. Filial divisions.
- B. Fulminant devised.
- C. Fearful hesitancy.
- D. Full deceit.
III. Filial Deception.
- A. Background of lies.
- B. Continuation in lies.
- C. Lies in words and deeds.
IV. Anguish of the frustrated.
- A. Doubly supplanted.
- B. Doubtful blessing.
- C. Dubious relief.
V. Anger reigns.
- A. Son of Cain.
- B. Intrigue lives on.
- C. Paternal assent sought.

CHAPTER 28

I. Family projection.
- A. Canaanite unacceptable.
- B. Blessing amplified.
- C. Two phase logic.
  1. Fear of brotherly retaliation.
  2. Filial obedience.
- D. Futile Esau.
II. A night of uncertainty.
- A. Separated from the familiar.
- B. Separated from home comforts.
- C. Separated from earth's reality.
- D. Separated from misdirection.
- E. Separated from the secular.
III. A day of resolves.
- A. Recognition of God in nearness.
- B. Recognition of God in memorial.
- C. Recognition of God in place name.
- D. Recognition of God in vow.
  1. Condition.
  2. Committal.
  3. Consecration

CHAPTER 29

I. Journey's end.
- A. Well of water
- B. Information.
- C. Instruction.
- D. Introduction.
II. Joining family.
- A. Bargained relationship.
- B. Joy in service.
- C. Supplanter supplanted.
- D. Double dealing.
III. Family expansion.
- A. Fecundity.
- B. Frustration.
- C. Family history in names.

CHAPTER 30

I. Denied motherhood.
- A. Shifting blame.
- B. Impossible demands.
- C. False hopes.
- D. Vicarious claims.
II. Imitating motherhood.
- A. Power of example.
- B. Vicarious victory.
- C. Bargaining powers.
III. The reality of motherhood.
- A. Psychiatric import.
- B. The real power of procreation.
- C. Genuine joy.

- IV. Climatic aspects of motherhood.
  - A. The pull of the homeland.
  - B. Economic demands.
  - C. Changed wage scale.
- V. Banal response to motherhood.
  - A. Favorable increase planned.
  - B. Primitive genetics.
  - C. Superior supplanter.

CHAPTER 31

- I. Frowning fraternity.
  - A. Frustrating filiations.
  - B. Fulminating faces.
  - C. Fatherland invitation.
    1. Deity directed.
    2. Bountiful blessings.
- II. Occidental counseling.
  - A. Wives included.
  - B. Wives informed.
  - C. Wives weaned.
- III. Prestidigitating pilgrimage.
  - A. Subtle departure.
  - B. Not a hoof left behind.
  - C. All bridges burned.
- IV. Paternal pursuit.
  - A. Multiple reasons.
    1. Blood ties.
    2. Property loss.
    3. Stolen idols.
  - B. Warning dream.
  - C. Recognized fatherland appeal.
  - D. Fruitless search.
- V. Filial flailings.
  - A. Ignorant pride.
  - B. Chiding spirit.
  - C. Useless review.
- VI. Patriarchal claims.
  - A. Power of kinship.
  - B. Exaggerated sense of ownership.
  - C. Safety in bargaining.
  - D. Material evidence.
  - E. Evidence in nomenclature.
  - F. Worship included.
  - G. "Sweet sorrow" in parting.

CHAPTER 32

- I. Divine welcome committee.
  - A. Recognized.
  - B. Presaged division in place name.
  - C. Invitation to welcome.
- II. Aroused fear.
  - A. Over-welcome foreboded.
  - B. Strategy in division.
  - C. Humility in prayer.
  - D. Reason in remembrance.
- III. Gift strategy.
  - A. Value in intervals.
  - B. Announcements for anticipation.
  - C. Journey safety measure.
- IV. Prevailing petition.
  - A. Alone in struggle.
  - B. Conditional release.
  - C. Name significance.
    1. Change matched with character.
    2. Place named as experience.
    3. No reciprocity in exchange.
    4. Perpetuate experience in custom.

CHAPTER 33

- I. Division in reality.
  - A. Present danger.
  - B. Conscience motivation.
  - C. Paternal graduations.
  - D. Personal safety unimportant.

GENESIS

  II. Reunion in family ties.
      A. Animosity absent.
      B. Courteous introductions.
      C. Understanding through gifts.
      D. Protection declined.
      E. Amiable separation.
      F. Neighbors, not domestic inmates.
  III. Established home.
      A. Legal possession.
      B. Permanent dwelling.
      C. Worship continued.

CHAPTER 34

  I. The way of the flesh.
      A. Hospitality.
      B. Humanism.
      C. Humiliation.
  II. The loss of flesh.
      A. Subtle bargaining.
      B. Selfish assentation.
      C. Soulless promises.
  III. Insensible flesh.
      A. Revenge motivation.
      B. Regardless of consequences.
      C. Rampant spoilation.
      D. Residence removal.

CHAPTER 35

  I. God's nearness.
      A. Clear directions.
      B. Full return.
      C. Duo cleanup.
      D. Complete separation.
      E. A blessing of fear.
  II. The strength of Bethel.
      A. In worship.
      B. In name change.
      C. In time of grief.
      D. In iterated covenant.
      E. In memorial.
  III. Family sorrow.
      A. Sorrow in travail.
      B. Perpetuated in name.
      C. Broken family circle.
      D. A son's indiscretion.
      E. Paternal passing

CHAPTER 36

  I. Edom's family tree.
      A. Isaac's favorite.
      B. Canaanite marriages.
      C. Ishmael tie-in.
      D. Itinerary in riches.
  II. Edom's history.
      A. Inter-inner marriages.
      B. Titles of leadership.
      C. Eleven branches.

CHAPTER 37

  I. Filial favoritism.
      A. Paternal loyalty.
      B. Paternal prejudice.
      C. Patrimonial perplexity.
      D. Psychological pride.
          1. Dream compensation.
          2. Repetition in exaltation.
      E. Paternal rebuke.
  II. Division of labor.
      A. Herdsmen.
      B. Messenger.
      C. Neighborly help.
  III. Fraternal fulminations.
      A. Jealous plans.
      B. Subtrafuge of conscience.
      C. Envious action.
      D. Selfish profit motive.
  IV. Fulfillment complete.
      A. Ishmael's promises.
      B. Paternal conclusion.
      C. Perpetuity in grief.
      D. Egyptian sojourn presaged.

CHAPTER 38

I. Family tree limb.
   A. The Judah branch.
   B. The Judah twig.
   C. The Judah leaves.
      1. Leaves fall.
      2. Leaves protected.
      3. Leaves neglected.
II. A woman's way.
   A. Sociological strategy.
   B. Sociological risk.
   C. Sociological disclosure.
   D. Sociological acknowledgment.
III. Progeny replacements.
   A. Two sons lost.
   B. Two sons gained.
   C. Primogenture precedent?

CHAPTER 39

I. Blessing in slavery?
   A. Immediate results only.
   B. Temptation of success.
   C. Prosperity perils.
   D. Temptation in comeliness.
II. Integrity in slavery.
   A. Material limitations.
   B. Moral limitations.
   C. Maturity in confrontations.
III. Insidiousness in slavery.
   A. Frustration in futility.
   B. False accusation.
   C. Misused evidence.
   D. Partially believed report.
   E. Incarceration increased.
   F. Continued blessings.

CHAPTER 40

I. The land of dreams.
   A. Limitless domain of dreams.
   B. Limited knowledge about dreams.
   C. Right interpreter of dreams.
II. The promises of dreams.
   A. Restoration.
   B. Renunciation.
   C. Remembrance?

CHAPTER 41

I. Dreams in high places.
   A. The Pharaoh included.
   B. Duo-emphasis.
   C. Troubled mind.
   D. Futile dependence
II. Remembrance in high places.
   A. Self-rebuke of Pharaoh's butler.
   B. Revelation of experience.
III. Invitation of high places.
   A. The king's call.
   B. The prisoner's preparation.
   C. Report of rumor.
IV. Humility in high places.
   A. Honor to whom honor is due.
   B. The Pharaoh's limitation.
   C. Pharaoh's prophetic dreams.
   D. Unity in message.
   E. Surety of message.
   F. Present application.
V. Honor in high places.
   A. Position.
   B. Proprietary.
   C. Plighted troth.
   D. Paraded authority.
   E. Provisions in plenty.
   F. Predicament of famine.

CHAPTER 42

I. Merchandising in famine.

GENESIS

    A. Patriarchal authority.
    B. Patriarchal withholding.
    C. Patriarchal obedience.
II. Remembrance in famine.
    A. Dreams recalled.
    B. Recognition one-sided.
    C. Testing accusation.
    D. Proof demanded.
    E. Alteration in proof.
    F. Guilty consciences revived.
III. Magnanimity in famine.
    A. Grain sold to "spies."
    B. Money returned in sacks.
    C. Return provisions provided.
    D. Hostage required.
IV. Reporting in famine.
    A. Self-vindication.
    B. Limitations on subsequent trips.
    C. Patriarchal blame.

CHAPTER 43

I. Famine pressure.
    A. Food demand.
    B. Futile reasoning.
    C. Father-image and blame.
II. Family pressure.
    A. Fraternal surety.
    B. Time element.
    C. Economic strategy.
    D. Reverent plea.
III. Heart pressure.
    A. Social invitations.
    B. Offer of restitution.
    C. Brothers united.
    D. National restriction.
    E. Occult seating.
    F. Test by portions.

CHAPTER 44

I. Planned fraternal test.
    A. Planted evidence.
    B. Pursuit of blame.
    C. Palaver of innocency.
    D. Pledge of restoration.
II. Pledged fraternal loyalty.
    A. Another fulfillment of dreams.
    B. Another instance of ring-leadership.
    C. Anguished review.
    D. Autotelic substitute offer.

CHAPTER 45

I. Fraternal revelation.
    A. Fraternally troubled minds.
    B. Frustrated family viewpoint.
    C. Futile self-blame.
    D. Fulfilled Abrahamic promise.
II. Fraternal invitation.
    A. Divine purpose.
    B. Designed migration.
    C. Delight in reunion.
III. Pharaoh's endorsement.
    A. Full collaboration.
    B. Favorable offer of assistance.
    C. Fulgent replacements promised.
IV. Further fraternal testing.
    A. Abundant gifts.
    B. Partiality to Benjamin.
    C. Paternal diffidence.
    D. Warning against jealousy.
V. Flabbergasting report.
    A. Unbelief's assertion.
    B. Belief's ascent.
    C. Resolve's reign.

CHAPTER 46

I. Migration patterns.
    A. Complete move.

B. Worship at point of separation.
   C. Covenant renewal.
II. Migration personnel.
   A. Complete families.
   B. Roster by sons' names.
   C. Genealogy census.
III. Migration particularities.
   A. Message of arrival.
   B. Guide to assigned place.
   C. Tender reunion.
   D. Occupational separation.
   E. Preparation for court presentation.

CHAPTER 47

I. Migration report.
   A. Representative presentation.
   B. Polite reception.
   C. Patriarchal blessing to Pharaoh.
   D. Regal approval for location.
II. Famine progress.
   A. Bread for money.
   B. Bread for livestock.
   C. Bread for land.
   D. Bread for manpower.
   E. Church land exemption.
III. Famine termination.
   A. Seed for planting.
   B. Precedent rental scale.
   C. Alien prosperity.
   D. Paternal-filial agreement.

CHAPTER 48

I. Paternal infirmity.
   A. A favorite son's visit.
   B. Grandsons included.
   C. Reminiscence of promise.
   D. Acknowledge of fulfillment.
II. Paternal adoption.
   A. Grandsons in egalitarian claim.
   B. Limited vision.
   C. Desire to bless.
III. Paternal supplanting.
   A. Second-born in first place.
   B. First-born also in future.
   C. Favoritism still.

CHAPTER 49

I. Patriarchal prognosticating.
   A. Paternal insights.
   B. Foresight by hindsight.
   C. Rulership designated.
   D. Judicial powers recognized.
   E. Internal strife present.
   F. Strength over jealousy.
   G. Social maturity.
II. Patriarchal passing.
   A. Blessings complete.
   B. Pledged filial compliance.
   C. Interment instructions.
   D. Submission to inevitability.

CHAPTER 50

I. Preparation by preferment.
   A. Appropriate grief.
   B. National customs followed.
   C. Deference in permission.
II. Pledge to father kept.
   A. Courteous attendants.
   B. Immediate family present.
   C. Homeland mourning period.
   D. Canaanitish recognition in sincerity.
   E. Completed mission.
III. Conscience aftermath.

EXODUS

A. Patriarchal restraints gone.
B. Diplomatic approach.
C. Humble apology offered.
D. Dreams fulfilled again.
E. Proper perspective.
F. Fraternal tranquility.

IV. Pharaoh's progeny.
   A. Posterity.
   B. Promises to fathers believed.
   C. Pledges for temporary burial.

EXODUS

CHAPTER 1

I. Hebrew background.
   A. Genealogy reviewed.
   B. Divine sanctioned prosperity.
   C. Change of authority.
II. Hebrew status change.
   A. Possible strength direction.
   B. Rigor decimation projected.
   C. Power of stamina.
III. Hebrew limitation.
   A. Alarming increase.
   B. Thwarted limitations.
   C. Humanity's response.
   D. Divine sanction.
   E. Extension of limitations.

CHAPTER 2

I. Leadership background.
   A. Progeny of epitome of anger.
   B. Power of mother love.
      1. Defiant deception.
      2. Subtle strategy.
      3. Careful concern.
      4. Training in traditions.
II. Leadership preparation.
   A. Nationality revealed.
   B. Vicarious sonship.
   C. School advantages (Acts 7:22).
III. Leadership undirected.
   A. National spirit pressure.
   B. Irrational action.
   C. Projection into personal matters.
   D. Power of gossips.
IV. Leadership in flight.
   A. Adoption security missing.
   B. Nearest refuge.
   C. Courteous helpfulness.
   D. Hospitable reception.
   E. Family "adoption."
V. Leadership in unknown readiness.
   A. Change of king.
   B. Bondage grievances.
   C. Covenant recall.
   D. Divine recognition.

CHAPTER 3

I. Leadership's call.
   A. Regular activities.
   B. Spectacular phenomenon.
   C. Attention gained.
   D. Sacred spot.
   E. Face to face with God.
II. Leadership's commission.
   A. Deity's recognition in review.

B. Covenant conditions.
C. Orders of the *day*.
III. Leadership's objections.
   A. Humility.
   B. Disbelief.
      1. In Deity's presence.
      2. In credence of Israel.
IV. Leadership's proof.
   A. Review of return to Horeb.
   B. Power of Deity's name.
   C. Corroboration with Israel's elders.
   D. Reactions in summary.
   E. Retribution results.

CHAPTER 4

I. Leadership's hesitation.
   A. Obstinate reception.
   B. Predictable call for proof.
   C. Proof offer.
      1. Animated material object.
      2. Physical infirmity.
      3. Chemical metamorphosis.
   D. Lack of fluency.
II. Leadership's assurance.
   A. Creator's powers.
   B. Anger's support.
   C. Vicarious assistance.
   D. Signs for confirmation.
III. Leadership's reconnaissance.
   A. Patriarchal consent.
   B. Divine reassurance.
   C. Recognition of God's Family.
   D. Dalliance of ordinance.
   E. Mother-love revolt.
IV. Leadership's report.
   A. Bolstered strength.
   B. Israel's acceptance.

CHAPTER 5

I. Leadership's plea.
   A. As divinely given.
   B. To proper authority.
   C. No recognition of Deity.
II. Leadership athwart.
   A. Accusation of "picketing."
   B. Labor rigors increased.
      1. Straw withheld.
      2. Work quotas increased.
      3. Complaints fruitless.
   C. Short vision of freedom donees.
   D. Accusation of failure.

CHAPTER 6

I. Victorious promises.
   A. Belief, the first requirement.
   B. Recall of fidelity.
   C. New name significance.
   D. Specific covenant.
II. Spurned promises.
   A. People with deaf ears.
   B. People with shortsighted eyes.
   C. Discouraged spokesman.
   D. Isaianic limitations.
III. Genealogical promises.
   A. Family lineage.
   B. Identity of spokesman.
   C. Reiterated directives.
   D. Reiterated incapability.

CHAPTER 7

I. Vicarious divinity.
   A. Power and prophet.
   B. Faithful mouthpiece.
   C. Postponed success.
   D. Purpose stated.
   E. Faithful in action.

II. Power display.
   A. Progression of signs.
   B. Matching necromancy.
   C. Magic limited.
   D. Seeing — but not believing.
III. Projected power.
   A. Pharaoh followed.
   B. Another chance to comply.
   C. National lifeline altered at altar.
      1. Loathsome water.
      2. River life destroyed.
      3. Enchantment response.
   D. Stubborn heart.
   E. Complete duration.

CHAPTER 8

I. Continued plea.
   A. Ever present alternative.
   B. Universal contamination.
   C. Fulfillment as predicted.
   D. Magical counter part.
II. Expedient superficial assent.
   A. Conditional bargain.
   B. Time element.
   C. Answered prayer of Moses.
   D. Royal renege.
III. Continued plagues.
   A. Dust to lice.
   B. Magical incompetence.
      1. Failure.
      2. Right testimony.
      3. Royal obstinacy.
   C. Flies by swarms.
   D. Peculiar separateness.
   E. Limited assent.
   F. Impossible compliance.
   G. Altered limitations.
   H. Divine response.
   I. Regal re-negation.

CHAPTER 9

I. Renewed requests.
   A. Material depletion promised.
   B. Israel property spared.
   C. Timed schedule.
   D. Obduracy remains.
   E. Physical infirmity.
      1. Man and beast victimized.
      2. Magicians included.
II. Promised plague completion.
   A. Remedy in yielding.
   B. All as proof of Deity.
   C. Meteorological disturbance.
   D. Land of Goshen spared.
III. Quasi-humility.
   A. Lip-service.
   B. Learning experience.
   C. Lacking real repentance.
   D. Late harvest possible.
   E. Living rebellion.

CHAPTER 10

I. Duo-purpose in experiences.
   A. Proof to Pharaoh
   B. Posterity's spiritual education.
   C. Progression in plagues.
   D. Plea of Pharaoh's princes.
II. Negotiation attempts.
   A. Personal commitment.
   B. Spokesman expelled.
   C. Locusts called.
   D. Verdure removed.
III. Limited remorse.
   A. Immediate forgiveness.
   B. Limited prayer.
   C. Ephemeral agreement.
IV. Light withheld.
   A. Abject darkness.

B. Objective submission limits?
  C. Complete withdrawal needed.
  D. Denied audience.

CHAPTER 11

I. Final plague soon.
  A. Last chance favors.
    1. Favorable reception.
    2. Profuse borrowings.
  B. Last warning to Pharaoh.
II. Final prediction.
  A. No exemptions among Egyptians.
  B. No favorable response.
  C. Interview ended in anger.
  D. Mental preparation.

CHAPTER 12

I. The month of beginnings.
  A. Revised calendar.
  B. Preparation for exemption.
  C. Conservation measures.
  D. Complete observance.
  E. Restricted procedures.
II. The journey of beginnings.
  A. Ready to travel.
  B. The sign of sacrifice.
  C. Freedom in compliance.
III. The ordinance of beginnings.
  A. The way of deliverance.
  B. The way of favoritism fulfilled.
  C. The way of remembrance.
  D. The way of teaching.
IV. The obedience in beginnings.
  A. Full compliance.
  B. The visitant in the night.
  C. All unprotected visited.
V. The freedom in beginnings.
  A. Thrust upon Israel.
  B. Prayer interest sought.
  C. Full-handed departure.
VI. The history in beginnings.
  A. National census.
  B. Years of Egyptian habitation.
  C. Perpetuated remembrances.
  D. Personal restrictions.

CHAPTER 13

I. Firstborn redemption.
  A. God's right by exemption.
  B. Man and beast application.
  C. Perpetual reminders.
    1. Redemption.
    2. Ordinance observation.
    3. Teaching value.
    4. Phylacteries.
II. The route of redemption.
  A. Bypass war possibilities.
  B. Coastal route.
  C. Fulfilled pledge.
  D. Around the clock guidance.
  E. Duo-protection.

CHAPTER 14

I. Pharaoh's last lesson.
  A. Ease of pursuit.
  B. Heart-bent pursuit.
  C. Preparation of pursuit.
II. Israel's fear.
  A. Human logic.
  B. Begrudged obedience.
  C. Lips of faith.
III. Israel's orders.
  A. Fixed position and mind.
  B. God's presence.
  C. Promised lesson for Israel and Egypt.

EXODUS

IV. Israel's protection.
   A. Light and separation.
   B. Sea passage.
   C. Sea in vengeance.
   D. Faith by sight.

CHAPTER 15

I. The song of deliverance.
   A. Divine strength recognized.
   B. Lip devotion.
   C. Human appraisal.
   D. Natural control with God.
   E. Lesson to be learned.
II. The dance of victory.
   A. Women of Israel only.
   B. Song accompaniment.
III. Subsequent travels.
   A. Away from sea.
   B. Bitter water.
   C. Empirical lessons.
   D. Adequate camp facilities.

CHAPTER 16

I. Murmuring Israel.
   A. Forgotten providence.
   B. Emphasis on immediate lack.
   C. Blind doubts.
II. Day-by-day needs.
   A. Daily application.
   B. Provision for Seventh Day.
   C. Proof of providence.
III. Murmuring multitude.
   A. Opposition to God.
   B. Promised answers.
     1. Glory of the Lord revealed.
     2. Meat in abundance.
     3. Bread from "heaven" (cf. John 6:32ff.)
        a. Of the earth.
        b. Given by the Father.
        c. Via natural phenomenon, the dew.
IV. Stubborn reluctance.
   A. Daily chore.
   B. Egalitarian measure.
   C. Spoilage in violation of Divine decree.
   D. Hunger in violation of Divine decree.
V. Memorial exception.
   A. Saved sample spared.
   B. Posterity's perception.

CHAPTER 17

I. Thirst of throats, not souls.
   A. Short memories.
   B. Constant complainers.
   C. Consternation of consorts.
II. Water for wantonness.
   A. The voice of authority.
   B. The rod of action.
III. Amalek antagonism.
   A. Force meets force.
   B. The rod of victory.
   C. Human frailties.
   D. Brotherly bolstering.
   E. Israel's victory.
   F. Sealed doom for Amalek.

CHAPTER 18

I. Family reunion.
   A. Power of good report.
   B. Blood ties.
   C. Reciprocal admiration and respect.
II. Full report of deliverance.
   A. The Word of the Lord.
   B. The glory to the Lord.
   C. The worship of the Lord.

III. Fatherly advice.
    A. Burden of judgments.
    B. Undelegated judgments.
    C. Divine sanction of judgment division.
    D. Proof in practice.

CHAPTER 19

I. The return to Sinai.
    A. Israel's camp before the Lord.
    B. Review of protective measures.
    C. Preparation for life pattern.
    D. Conditional continuation.
II. Lip-loyalty.
    A. Fresh memories.
    B. Preparation for proclamation.
    C. Restricted auditorium.
III. Awesome appearance.
    A. Audience ready.
    B. Two-way communication.
    C. Mountain meeting
    D. Precaution for preservation.
    E. Egoism boasts.
    F. Humble obedience.

CHAPTER 20

I. The pattern for worship.
    A. Reverence for Deity's being.
    B. Reverence for Deity's person.
    C. Reverence for Deity's name.
    D. Reverence for Deity's day.
II. The pattern for society.
    A. Sacredness of filial relationship.
    B. Sacredness of human life.
    C. Sacredness of moral standards.
    D. Sacredness of property.
    E. Sacredness of integrity.
    F. Sacredness of stewardship.
III. The pattern of communication.
    A. Awe and fear.
    B. Go-between desired.
    C. Spiritual enlightenment possible.
IV. The pattern for altar.
    A. Terrestrial.
    B. Unhewn.
    C. Humble position.

CHAPTER 21

I. The judgment on servitude.
    A. Service period limited.
    B. Status preserved.
    C. Subservience voluntary.
    D. Successive provision.
II. The judgment of betrothals.
    A. Integrity protected.
    B. Sustenance maintained.
    C. Freedom possible.
III. The judgment for homicides.
    A. Life for a life.
    B. Cities of refuge.
    C. No exemption in guilt.
IV. The judgment for health insurance.
    A. Pay for time loss.
    B. No ownership exemptions.
    C. Freedom for partial disabilities.
    D. By-stander coverage.
V. The judgment for losses by beasts.
    A. Ownership responsibility.
    B. Limited liability for strays.
    C. Degrees of payment.
    D. Unprotected pits.

EXODUS

    E. Liability according to guilt.

CHAPTER 22

I. The guilt of theft.
    A. Restoration ratio.
    B. Forfeit of life.
        1. Death in apprehension.
        2. Death in act of theivery.
        3. Life in slavery.
    C. No squatter's rights.
II. Careless arson.
    A. Innocent beginning
    B. Restitution required.
III. Security risks.
    A. Custodial responsibility.
    B. Liability by judgment.
    C. Proof of innocence.
    D. Borrower's responsibility.
IV. Social responsibility.
    A. Moral integrity.
    B. Honorable reactions.
    C. Witchcraft condemned.
    D. Sexual perversion forbidden.
    E. Devout Theistic worship demanded.
    F. Good neighbor policy required.
        1. No selfish oppression allowed.
        2. Benevolence in lending money.
    G. No reviling in religion or politics.
    H. Punctuality in stewardship.
    I. Separated by manner of life.

CHAPTER 23

V. Evil leadership dangers.
    A. Truthless gossiping dangerous.
    B. Evil intents anathema.
    C. Frugal restraints.
    D. Neighborliness in practice.
    E. Discretionary implications.
VI. Material gains danger.
    A. Bribery or gift discoloration.
    B. Selfish oppression evil.
    C. Agrarian practice violations.
    D. Bedimmed worship values.
VII. Worship neglect dangers.
    A. Annual feasts oversight.
    B. Stewardship in first fruits omission.
    C. Undecided manpower.
    D. Indifference in details.
VIII. Leadership awareness.
    A. Angel guide.
        1. Alert obedience required.
        2. Forgiveness only with God.
    B. Loyalty in commitment.
    C. Health and prosperity in obedience.
    D. Conquest success.
        1. Gradual, but sure.
        2. Land control necessary.
    E. Separateness.

CHAPTER 24

I. Mountaintop invitation
    A. Selective guest list.
    B. Full report of legal proclamation.
    C. Obedience promised.

    D. Record made.
    E. Covenant sealed in blood.
 II. Mountaintop journey.
    A. Moses and elders of Israel.
    B. God's presence recognized.
    C. Pact sealed in fellowship.
III. Mountaintop experience.
    A. Moses alone with God.
    B. Permanent record promised.
    C. God's glory visible to all.
    D. Meeting on the Lord's day.
    E. No week-end revival time.

CHAPTER 25

  I. The call for stewardship response.
    A. Voluntary.
    B. Materials.
       1. Metals
       2. Fabrics.
       3. Hides and leather.
       4. Wood.
       5. Oil and spices.
       6. Precious stones.
 II. The use of stewardship response.
    A. Sanctuary of Jehovah.
    B. A dwelling for Jehovah.
    C. The pattern given.
III. The action of stewardship response.
    A. Complete plans.
    B. Specific articles.
       1. Ark of the covenant.
          a. Materials.
          b. Transportable.
          c. Connotative import.
             (1) Law within.
             (2) Witnessing evidence.
             (3) Under mercy seat.
             (4) God's presence.
       2. Showbread table.
       3. Candlestick
       4. Dishes and vessels.

CHAPTER 26

  I. Tabernacle wall curtains.
    A. Harmony in color.
    B. Uniform accuracy.
    C. Unity in construction.
 II. Tabernacle roof coverings.
    A. Durable skins.
    B. Workable sizes.
    C. Draping trim.
    D. Multiple protection.
III. Tabernacle timbers.
    A. Wall and corner supports.
    B. Definite dimensions.
    C. Adequate joints.
 IV. Tabernacle veil.
    A. Matching color scheme.
    B. Supports provided.
    C. Separating purpose.
  V. Tabernacle divisions.
    A. Most holy place.
       1. Ark of testimony.
       2. Mercy seat.
    B. The holy place.
       1. Without the veil.
       2. The candlestick.
       3. The showbread table.
       4. Appurtenances positioned.
 VI. The tabernacle door.
    A. Fabric harmony.
    B. Timber supports.
    C. Metallic fasteners.

EXODUS

CHAPTER 27

I. The altar for worship.
   A. Regular rectangular size.
   B. Distinct markings.
   C. Worship vessels in matching metal.
   D. Portable provisions.
      1. Construction pattern
      2. Carrying devices.
II. The area for worship.
   A. Before the tent of meeting.
   B. Screening curtain walls.
   C. Timber supports.
   D. Definite dimensions.
   E. Gate closure.
III. The oil for worship.
   A. Candlestick lights.
   B. Anointing supply later.

CHAPTER 28

I. The priests for worship.
   A. Family designated.
   B. Priests' appearance.
      1. Glory.
      2. Beauty.
II. The priests' wardrobe for worship.
   A. Craftsmen's call.
   B. Craftsmen instructed.
   C. Craftsmen designated.
III. The breastplate for worship.
   A. Symbol of judgment.
   B. Gems for the 12 tribes.
   C. To be worn by chief priest.
   D. Continual practice.
IV. The priestly robe for worship.
   A. Decorative color and trim.
   B. Sound for reverence.
   C. Plated mitre.
   D. Worship significance.
V. Priestly garments for worship.
   A. Complete wardrobes.
   B. Consecrated for worship.
   C. Required for holiness import.

CHAPTER 29

I. Priestly anointing.
   A. Vicarious atonement.
   B. Consecration meal menu.
   C. Ceremonial cleansing.
   D. Ceremonial clothing.
   E. Ceremonial anointing.
   F. Vicarious identity
   G. The blood applied.
   H. Altar fires — within, without camp.
II. Priestly sacrifices.
   A. Lamb identity.
   B. Lamb offering.
   C. Personal dedication.
   D. Individual anointing.
   E. Holy garments in succession.
   F. Fellowship feast.
   G. Remnants of feast inviolate.
III. Priestly duties in worship.
   A. Atonement for artifacts.
      1. Atonement time set.
      2. Atonement method.
   B. Daily experience.
IV. Deity's acceptance.
   A. Meeting place.
   B. Sanctified sanctuary.
   C. Sanctified priesthood.
   D. Abiding presence.
   E. Spiritual enlightenment possible.

CHAPTER 30

I. The altar of incense.

A. Matching pattern with offering altar.
   B. In holy place without the veil.
   C. Daily use, morning and evening.
   D. Inviolate use always.
   E. Special yearly use.
II. The official census.
   A. Soul ransoms.
   B. Uniformity-egalitarian.
   C. Dedicated service of gifts.
III. The vessels for cleansing.
   A. Lasting material.
   B. Convenient location.
   C. Ceremonial use.
IV. Anointing oil recipe.
   A. Spices that preserve.
      1. Preserve present status.
      2. Expel disturbing efforts.
      3. Repel destroying forces.
      4. Insure pleasant experiences.
   B. The oil of "gladness."
      1. Plentiful supply.
      2. Common commodity.
      3. Universal usage.
   C. Restricted application.
   D. Consecration power.
V. The perfume of perfection.
   A. Specified spices.
   B. Specified service.
   C. Divine devotion.

CHAPTER 31

I. The call for service.
   A. Designated men of talents.
   B. Designing skills.
   C. Denotative accomplishments.
II. The call for separation.
   A. Consecrated use of time.
   B. Following Deity's example.
   C. Warning for violations.
III. The two tables of testimony.
   A. Proof of palaver.
   B. Complete communication.

CHAPTER 32

I. Inspiration by exposure only.
   A. Heathen background.
   B. Transient faith.
   C. Short memories.
II. Human expediency.
   A. Ear ornaments from dull ears.
   B. Fashioned by hand.
   C. Broken commandment.
   D. Faulty worship.
   E. Hoopla (Hootenanny).
III. Divine expulsion.
   A. Disowned people.
   B. Disclosed apostasy.
   C. Diagnosed malady.
   D. Declaimed substitute.
   E. Denied blessing.
IV. Vicarious intercession.
   A. Blindness of wrath.
   B. Disowned power.
   C. Acknowledged defeat.
   D. Covenant recall.
   E. Answered prayer.
V. Faulty practice.
   A. Reporting leader.
   B. Orientated leader.
   C. Ranting leader.
      1. Destroyed tables of testimony.
      2. Retributive measures.
      3. Personal application.
   D. Responsibility demanding leader.

       E. Face-saving explanation.
VI. Called-out loyalty.
       A. The Lord's own.
       B. Ready for action.
       C. Consecration for the task.
VII. Declaration of guilt.
       A. Offer of intercession.
       B. Intercessory prayer.
       C. Communal identity in condemnation.
       D. Individual indictment.
       E. Retained leadership duty.
       F. Punishment promised.

CHAPTER 33

I. Marching orders renewed.
       A. Covenant requirements.
       B. Angel protector and guide.
       C. Land worth claiming.
       D. Protective absence.
II. Mourning remorse.
       A. Guilt complex
       B. Ornaments of pride renounced.
       C. Damocles sword of danger.
III. The tent of meeting.
       A. Without the camp.
       B. Audience with God.
       C. Reverence for leadership.
       D. Evidence of God's presence.
       E. Direct communication.
       F. Continuous concourse.
IV. Reciprocal communication.
       A. Plea for pledge sign.
       B. Plea for complete cognizance.
       C. Pledged presence.
       D. Peculiar particular.
       E. Partial revelation.
              1. Human limitations.
              2. Divine love spares.

CHAPTER 34

I. Replacement tables of stone.
       A. Man's responsibility.
       B. God's rewriting promise.
       C. Proclamation of Deity's attributes.
       D. Worship in prayer.
II. Covenant review.
       A. Evidence of Divine protection.
              1. Obedience of Israel.
              2. Loyalty of Israel.
              3. Victories of Israel.
       B. Removal of snares.
              1. By-pass heathen examples.
              2. Forego heathen invitations.
                     a. To worship.
                     b. To socialize.
                     c. Idol manufacturing.
       C. Established patterns of worship.
              1. Kept feasts.
              2. Dedicated or redeemed firstborn.
       D. Stewardship of labor time.
III. Covenant terms available.
       A. Written copy.
       B. Precepts to be taught.
IV. The veil of glory.
       A. Close fellowship with Jehovah.
       B. Veiled to common view.

CHAPTER 35

I. A worship in time.
       A. Obligation to labor.
       B. Obligation to rest.
              1. Set pattern.
              2. Purposeful testimony.

- C. Pre-preparation.
- II. A worship by gifts.
  - A. All inclusive.
  - B. Voluntary.
  - C. Specified needs.
    1. Named materials.
    2. Designated uses.
  - D. A willing response.
- III. A worship by skills.
  - A. Spinning handcraft.
  - B. Called-out workmen.
    1. Endowed with skills.
    2. Dedicated talents.
  - C. Teaching program.
  - D. Designing skills.

CHAPTER 36

- I. Skills at work.
  - A. Craftsmanship.
  - B. Accounting department.
  - C. Total report.
    1. Daily records.
    2. Total computations.
  - D. Stewardship overplus.
- II. Pattern fulfillments.
  - A. Materials.
  - B. Dimensions.
  - C. Structural strengths.
  - D. Decorative features.
  - E. Portable provisions.

CHAPTER 37

- I. The Holiest of Holy appurtenance.
  - A. The Ark of the covenant.
  - B. Pattern perfection.
  - C. Mercy seat.
  - D. Symbols of God's presence.
  - E. Law under mercy.
- II. Holy place appurtenances.
  - A. Symbol of Spiritual food (table).
  - B. Symbols of preparation (vessels).
  - C. Symbol of spiritual light (lamp stand).
  - D. Symbol of spiritual communication (altar for incense).
  - E. Symbol of dedication (anointing oil).

CHAPTER 38

- III. Temple court appurtenances.
  - A. Altar of sacrifice.
  - B. Durable, but portable.
  - C. Court curtains.
    1. Beauty.
    2. Screening from the curious.
    3. Secure fastenings.
- IV. Workmen roster for all appurtenances.
  - A. Craftsmanship.
  - B. Widespread skills.
  - C. Reciprocal training.
- V. Offerings for appurtenance metals.
  - A. Accounting report (Audited). (Cf. chap. 36 I, B, C.)
  - B. Gifts by census count.
  - C. Egalitarian ratio (cf. chap. 30, II, B).
  - D. Sufficient amounts.

CHAPTER 39

- VI. Appurtenances in vestures.
  - A. Cloths of service.
    1. Priestly garments.
    2. High priest's breastplate.
       a. Jeweled for Israel's tribes.

LEVITICUS

   b. Symmetrically secured.
 B. Garments of distinction.
 C. Matching accouterments.
VII. Turnkey job completion.
 A. Full report to Moses.
 B. Pattern approval.

CHAPTER 40

I. Dedication service.
 A. Announced time.
 B. Pattern for assembling tabernacle.
 C. Dedication of tabernacle.
 D. Dedication of priesthood.
 E. Fully established as the pattern.
 F. Proof of Deity's presence.
 G. Pattern for progress.
  1. Rest in cloud's presence.
  2. Journey in cloud's presence.

LEVITICUS

CHAPTER 1

I. The burnt offering.
 A. From herd, flock, or fowl.
 B. Perfect male of herd or flock.
 C. Willing offering.
 D. Identity with offerer.
 E. Vicarious atonement.
 F. Priestly ministry.
 G. Specified manner.

CHAPTER 2

II. The meat (or meal) offering.
 A. Ingredients.
  1. Fine flour.
  2. Oil.
  3. Frankincense.
 B. Identity portion on altar.
 C. Priests' remnant.
 D. Various preparations.
  1. Baked in oven.
  2. Baked in frying pan.
 E. Free from leaven.
III. Firstfruits offering.
 A. No offering by fire.
 B. Salt seasoning for all offerings.
 C. Prepared by drying by fire.
 D. Identical with meat (meal) offering.
 E. Memorial by fire offering.
  1. Part of meal.
  2. Part of oil.
  3. All of frankincense.

CHAPTER 3

IV. The peace offering.
 A. Choice of source.
 B. Choice of sex of animal.
 C. Offering by fire.
 D. Identified with offerer.
 E. Perfect animal.
 F. Designated total by fire.
 G. Diet restrictions for Israel.

CHAPTER 4

V. Offering for sin through ignorance.
 A. Priest.

B. Congregation.
  1. Same offering.
  2. Same ritual.
     a. Vicarious identity.
     b. Blood applied.
     c. Burned without the camp.
C. Ruler.
  1. Male kid of the goats.
  2. Vicarious identity.
  3. Blood applied.
  4. Altar sacrifice.
D. Common people.
  1. Female kid or lamb.
  2. Vicarious identity.
  3. Blood applied.
  4. Altar sacrifice.

CHAPTER 5

VI. Offering for sin of uncleanness in word or deed.
  A. Concealed knowledge.
  B. Uncleanness in touch.
  C. Unclean in vows.
  D. Ignorance no excuse.
  E. Offering by possession status.
     1. Female lamb or kid.
     2. Two fowls.
     3. Measure of fine flour.
  F. Regular atonement pattern.
VII. Offering for trespassing in the sacred.
  A. Guilt in ignorance.
  B. Male sheep plus silver.
  C. Penalty portion added.
  D. Guilt in disobedience.

CHAPTER 6

VIII. Offering for trespass in falsehood.
  A. Violation of trust.
  B. Violation in fellowship.
  C. Violation in property rights.
  D. Violation by deceit.
  E. Penalty.
     1. Restitution.
     2. One-fifth value added.
     3. Regular trespass offering.
IX. Burnt offering ritual
  A. Priestly garments worn at altar.
  B. Continuous altar fire.
  C. Cleansing away of ashes.
  D. Cleansing completed in other garments.
X. Ritual of meat or meal offerings.
  A. Designated portion burned.
  B. Priests' portion eaten in tabernacle.
     1. Free from leaven.
     2. Dedicated use.
     3. Dedicating power.
  C. Offering by and for priests.
     1. Morning and evening worship.
     2. Perpetual ordinance.
     3. Completely burned.
  D. Offering for sin restrictions.
     1. Designated spot and manner.
     2. Duties of officiating priests.
     3. Destruction of earthen vessels.
     4. Designed cleansing practice.
     5. Dedicatory proclivities.

LEVITICUS

6. Demanded total burning.

CHAPTER 7

E. Trespass as sin.
   1. Same offering requirement.
   2. Same ritual.
   3. Same priest participation.
XI. Ritual for peace offering.
    A. Thanksgiving offering.
       1. Unleaven cakes with oil.
       2. Leavened bread.
       3. Animal sacrifice voluntary.
          a. Heave portion for priest.
          b. Blood applied.
          c. Consumed on day of offering.
    B. Offering for vows.
       1. Three day consumption period
       2. Residue burned.
       3. Penalty for disobedience.
    C. Excluded uncleanness.
       1. Unclean pollution burned.
       2. Personal unclean pollution penalized.
XII. Diet restrictions.
    A. Fat-free diet.
    B. Other uses for fats.
    C. Blood in diet excluded.
    D. Included fat in sacrifice.
    E. Priests' portions emphasized.
XIII. Summary of offering schedule.

CHAPTER 8

I. Consecration in preparation.
   A. Priests in person gathered.
   B. Priests' robes brought.
   C. Tabernacle and its contents.
   D. Congregation assembled to know.
   E. Obedience to God's commands.
   F. Priests appropriately robed.
II. Consecration in progress.
   A. Tabernacle anointing.
   B. Altar's sevenfold anointing.
   C. High priest's anointing.
   D. Priests' anointings.
III. Consecration by offerings.
   A. Priests' vicarious identity.
   B. Blood application.
      1. To altar horns.
      2. To high priest.
      3. To priests.
   C. Offering by fire.
      1. Bullock for sin.
         a. On altar for priests.
         b. Without the camp.
      2. Ram for burnt offering.
         a. Duplicated identity.
         b. Blood applied to altar.
         c. Complete consumption on altar.
      3. Ram for consecration.
         a. Repeated identity.

b. Blood applied on priests.
   c. Wave offering rituals.
   d. Moses included.
   e. Anointing oil with blood applied.
   f. Portions prepared and eaten.
   g. Any remnant consigned to fire.
IV. Consecration period of seven days.
   A. The Lord's requirements.
   B. The priests' obedience.

CHAPTER 9

I. The initial offering.
   A. Priests' offering first.
   B. Congregation of Israel present.
   C. Reminder of God's requirements.
   D. Atoned priests officiate.
II. The initial acceptance.
   A. Wave offering presented.
   B. Rituals completed.
   C. Priestly blessing.
   D. God's glory manifested.
   E. God's fire present.

CHAPTER 10

I. Strange fire.
   A. Pseudo worship.
      1. Right appurtenances.
      2. Wrong appurtenances.
      3. Beyond commandment.
   B. Fire of discipline.
      1. Divine source.
      2. Destruction of evil.
   C. Recognized purpose.
      1. Divine sanctity.
      2. Divine glory.
   D. Silent acquiesence.
   E. Removal of residue.
II. Continuing fire.
   A. Worship continued.
   B. Ministrations resumed.
   C. Priestly conduct augmented.
   D. Teaching responsibility.
   E. A family affair.
   F. Fire of anger burns.
   G. A father's heart throbs.

CHAPTER 11

I. Clean food.
   A. Clovenfooted ruminants.
   B. Finned with scales.
   C. Winged vegetarians with feet.
II. Unclean food.
   A. Clovenfooted nonruminants.
   B. Nonclovenfooted ruminants.
   C. Finless and scaleless.
   D. Carnivorous fowls.
   E. Scavenger fowls.
   F. Carnivorous insects.
   G. Rodent animals.
   H. Creeping animals — multipeds.
III. Contamination.
   A. The touch of the unclean.
   B. Contact with dead animals.
   C. Vicarious contacts.
IV. Decontamination.
   A. Ritualistic ablutions.
   B. Time lapse.
   C. Divine affinity.

LEVITICUS

CHAPTER 12

I. Purification for male birth.
  A. Time lapse set.
  B. Circumcision prescribed.
  C. Offerings required.
II. Purification for female birth.
  A. Double time lapse.
  B. No circumcision required.
  C. Burnt offering and sin offering required.
III. Offering capability variation.

CHAPTER 13

I. Uncleanness in flesh.
  A. Examined by priest.
  B. Quarantined by priest.
  C. Diagnosed by priest.
  D. Released or expelled by priest.
II. Uncleanness of hair of head or face.
  A. Examination.
  B. Probation period.
  C. Pronouncement.
III. Uncleanness in garments.
  A. Tests.
  B. Trials.
  C. Terminations.

CHAPTER 14

I. Leper cleansing.
  A. Separated from camp.
  B. Priest's examination.
  C. Cleansing ritual.
    1. Bird killed over running water
    2. Blood sprinkled.
    3. Released bird.
    4. Complete laundry.
    5. Complete shave.
    6. Complete bath.
    7. Entrance into camp.
    8. Denied access to tent.
    9. Another complete shave after seven days.
    10. Another complete laundry job.
    11. Another complete bath.
    12. Animals, oil, and meal offerings as to financial status.
      a. Trespass offering.
      b. Anointing and sprinkling of oil and blood.
      c. Sin offering.
      d. Burnt offering.
      e. Meat (meal) offering.
  D. Declaration of cleanness.
II. Housing cleansing.
  A. Report of need.
  B. Evacuation complete.
  C. Priest's inspection.
  D. Probation period of seven days.
  E. Reinspection.
  F. Replacement of contaminated materials.
  G. Complete renovation.
  H. Second reinspection.
  I. Condemnation for persistence.
  J. Demolished and removed.
  K. Contamination cleansed.
  L. Cleansed house spared.
  M. Cleansing ritual.
    1. A two bird offering.
    2. Similar procedure to that of man.
    3. Scapefowl released.
    4. Cleanness declared.

CHAPTER 15

I. Physical infirmity.
  A. Evidence diagnosis.
  B. Quarantine period.
  C. Quarantine of material contacts.
  D. Prevention of contagion.
II. Personal uncleanness.
  A. Personal hygiene.
  B. Wardrobe hygiene.
  C. Special feminine hygiene.
  D. Separation period.
  E. Cleansing practices.
III. Separation purposes.
  A. From uncleanness.
  B. From contagion.
  C. For right worship.

CHAPTER 16

I. Worship practice.
  A. Planned.
  B. Protected.
  C. Perpetual.
  D. Procedure.
    1. Selected offerings.
    2. Ceremonial cleansing.
    3. Sacerdotal garments.
    4. Sacerdotal atonement first.
II. Worship in vicarious offering.
  A. Presented before Jehovah by lot.
    1. The goat for sin offering.
    2. The goat for the wilderness.
  B. Annual incense before the Mercy Seat.
  C. Blood sprinkling before the Ark of the covenant.
  D. Altar application.
    1. Bullock.
    2. One goat.
  E. Scapegoat sent into the wilderness.
III. Worship on specified Sabbath.
  A. Sacerdotal ministry.
  B. Sacerdotal patrimony.

CHAPTER 17

I. Worship in established pattern.
  A. Precise presentation.
  B. Proper place.
  C. Personal identity.
  D. Punishment for perversion.
II. Worship for prescribed person.
  A. Separation from evil forms.
  B. No exemptions in personnel.
  C. Sacred exclusion.
  D. Food limitations.

CHAPTER 18

I. Between two fires.
  A. Egypt's evils.
  B. Canaan's evils.
  C. The way of life opened.
II. Moral integrity.
  A. Lewdness off limits.
  B. Inviolate near kin.
  C. Sex perversion out of bounds.
  D. Separated unto holiness.

CHAPTER 19

I. Personal integrity in worship.
  A. The call to holiness.
  B. The call for filial honor to parents.
  C. The call for full compliance.
II. Personal integrity in charity.
  A. Generosity in harvests.

LEVITICUS

    B. Recognition of property rights.
    C. Truthfulness in communication.
    D. Honesty in transactions.
    E. Concern for the handicapped.
    F. Equity in judgments.
    G. No place for gossiping.
    H. Actions motivated by *agape*.
III. Personal integrity in husbandry.
    A. No livestock propagation diversity.
    B. No diversity in planting fields.
    C. No domestic violations.
    D. Fruit harvest pattern set.
IV. Personal integrity in appearances.
    A. At meal time.
    B. Tonsorial limitations.
    C. No fleshly mutilations.
V. Personal integrity in community life.
    A. Inviolate feminine chastity.
    B. Sincerity in sabbatical observances.
    C. Reverence for place of worship.
    D. No dependence on magic.
    E. Honor for age.
    F. No discrimination for strangers.
    G. Standardized weights and measures.

CHAPTER 20

I. No human sacrifice.
    A. No fruit of body for sin of soul.
    B. Congregational judgment.
    C. No security in condoning acts.
    D. Divine judgment assured.
II. No human magic sanctions.
    A. Divine denunciation.
    B. Annihilation for offenders.
III. No human immorality unpunished.
    A. Wandering respect.
    B. Wandering desires.
    C. Wandering eyes.
IV. No human disobedience.
    A. All God's commandments binding.
    B. The sign of separation.
    C. Prosperity in obedience.
    D. Separateness, a reality.

CHAPTER 21

I. Priestly defilement defined.
    A. Restricted to consanguinity in death.
    B. No disfigurations.
    C. Recognition of holy office.
    D. Marital relation restrictions.
    E. Example of holy annointing.
II. Priestly family sanctity.
    A. Moral violations purged.
    B. Activities limited to duties.
III. Priestly physique blemishless.
    A. Official limitations.
    B. Sustenance inviolate

CHAPTER 22

I. Priestly status.
    A. Separated for duty.

- B. Separated things for worship.
- C. Separated from uncleanness.
- D. Separated from illness.
- E. Separated for indiscretion.
- F. Separated in familial response.

II. Priestly usurpation.
- A. Ignorance penalty.
- B. Sanctity of dedicated things.
- C. Didactic duties.

III. Priestly censorship.
- A. Judge of motivations.
- B. Judge of soundness of animal.
- C. Judge appropriateness of animal.
- D. Judge eligibility of offerer.
- E. Judge compliance with requirements.

IV. Priestly purpose.
- A. Witness to God's glory.
- B. Witness to God's motive.

CHAPTER 23

I. The law of labor.
- A. Six days for work.
- B. The seventh day for rest.
    1. No toil allowed.
    2. The Lord's Sabbath.

II. The law of stated worship.
- A. The Lord's Passover.
    1. Calendar designation.
    2. Feast ingredients.
    3. Sabbath convocations.
- B. The feast of harvest.
    1. First fruits offering to priests.
    2. Offerings.
        a. Wave sheaf.
        b. Perfect lamb of the first year.
        c. Meal (meat) offering.
        d. Offering before personal use.
- C. The feast of weeks.
    1. Pentecostal in time.
    2. Sabbatic beginning and end.
    3. Offering designation.
        a. Loaves of bread.
        b. Seven lambs.
        c. Two rams.
        d. One young bullock.
        e. One goat kid.
        f. Two yearling lambs.

III. The law of harvest.
- A. Residue for gleaning by the poor.
- B. Provisions for strangers.

IV. The law of feast of tabernacles.
- A. Sabbath beginning.
- B. Offering provision.
- C. Work restrictions.
- D. Binding on all.
- E. Seven days in seventh month.
- F. Reminder of wilderness wanderings.
- G. Witnessing testimony.

CHAPTER 24

I. The continual light.
- A. The lamp in the tabernacle.
- B. The lamp oil.

II. The continual bread.
- A. Recipe by measure.
- B. Cakes by number.
- C. Week by week dedication.

LEVITICUS

    D. Holy food for holy ministers in a holy place.
III. The continual judgment.
    A. Careless speech in anger.
    B. Confined for judgment.
    C. Conference with authority.
    D. Consigned to punishment.
IV. Continual life value.
    A. Life for a life.
    B. Injury for an injury.
    C. Restoration for the restorable.
    D. Universal application.

CHAPTER 25

I. The land sabbath.
    A. Six years of harvest.
    B. One year of land rest.
    C. Provisions for all.
II. The pentecost of national jubilee.
    A. Feast of tabernacle commencement.
    B. Restoration of property rights.
    C. Restoration of personal liberty.
    D. Determined usage schedules.
        1. Land value.
        2. Service price.
III. Prosperity in obedience.
    A. Dwelling in safety.
    B. Harvests of plenty.
    C. Land use without ownership.
    D. Possession in perpetuity.
IV. Redemption schedules.
    A. Family redemption rights.
    B. Redemption or jubilee release.
    C. Walled city limitations.
    D. Levitical privileges.
    E. Interest-free loans.
    F. Bond servant restrictions.
    G. Relationship with God.

CHAPTER 26

I. True worship blessings.
    A. Free from idolatry.
    B. Full obedience requirement.
    C. Seasonal weather.
    D. Full harvests.
    E. Dwelling in full security.
    F. Free from oppression.
    G. Victory in defense.
    H. Fruitful posterity.
    I. Abiding in God's presence.
II. Rebellious rejection curses.
    A. Soul pattern.
    B. Common terror.
    C. Comsuming diseases.
    D. God's disapproval pronounced.
    E. Enemy triumphs.
    F. Evil rulers.
    G. Multiple punishment for sins.
    H. Futile prayer experience.
    I. Fruitless harvests.
    J. Prey of wild beasts.
    K. Prevailing famine.
    L. Promised slavery.
    M. Possible repentance.
III. Covenant remembrance.
    A. Promise to fathers renewed.
    B. Reality of land sabbaths.
    C. Remembered in punishment.
    D. Covenant keeping God affirmed.

CHAPTER 27

I. Personal vow schedule.
   A. According to age and sex.
   B. Evaluation by authority.
II. Personal possessions offerings.
   A. Holy dedication.
   B. Exchanged rate doubled.
   C. Redeeming ratio.
III. Personal real estate vows.
   A. Binding vow.
   B. Ratio redemptions.
      1. According to market value.
      2. According to jubilee schedule.
      3. Permanent possession possible.
IV. Personal stewardship.
   A. Redemption ratio.
   B. Redemption restrictions.
      1. Holy status.
      2. No value exemptions.
      3. God's claim inviolate.

NUMBERS

CHAPTER 1

I. Organized for conquest.
   A. Tribal leaders designated.
   B. Induction census.
   C. Age limits for active service.
   D. Army size established.
II. Levitical exemptions.
   A. Free from census.
   B. Service schedule for the tabernacle.
      1. In journeyings.
      2. In camp.
   C. Levitical camp site locations.

CHAPTER 2

I. Camp pattern.
   A. Family groupings by family standards.
   B. Directional tribal groupings.
      1. East.
         a. Judah under captain Nahshon.
         b. Issachar under captain Nethanell.
         c. Zebulun under captain Eliab.
      2. South.
         a. Reuben under captain Elizur.
         b. Simeon under captain Shelumiel.
         c. Gad under captain Eliasaph.
      3. West.
         a. Ephraim under captain Elishama.
         b. Manasseh under captain Gamaliel.
         c. Benjamin under captain Abidan.
      4. North.
         a. Dan under captain Ahiezer.
         b. Asher under captain Pagiel.
         c. Naphtali under captain Ahira.

NUMBERS

  II. Camp obedience.
    A. Camp organization.
    B. Travel organization.

CHAPTER 3

I. Levitical dedication.
  A. Entire tribe of Levi presented.
  B. Priestly family of Aaron.
  C. Strangers excluded.

II. Levitical census.
  A. Replacements for firstborn.
  B. Organized for service.
    1. Family and duties of Gershon on the west.
      a. Under chief Eliasaph.
      b. Care of tent covering.
      c. Care of door and other hangings.
    2. Family and duties of Kohath on the south.
      a. Under chief Elizaphan
      b. Charge of ARK.
      c. Charge of all other furnishings.
    3. Eleazar as chief of chiefs.
    4. Family and duties of Merari — Mahlites — Mushites.
      a. Under chief Zuriel.
      b. Campsite northward.
      c. Care of all framework of tabernacle.
    5. Moses and family of Aaron eastward.
      a. Over-all care of all the tabernacle.
      b. Censure bureau.
  C. Firstborn of all Israel counted.
    1. Exceeded Levites.
    2. Redemption of overplus by money.
    3. Redemption for priestly family.

CHAPTER 4

I. Specific Kohathites directives.
  A. Service tenure established.
  B. Chief priest's preparatory duties.
    1. Veil sacred things from common eyes.
    2. Worship appurtenances protected.
  C. Profane touch eliminated by fear.

II. Specific priestly duties.
  A. Lamp oil.
  B. Sweet incense.
  C. Daily meal offering.
  D. Anointing oil.

III. Specific Gershonite directives.
  A. Service tenure established.
  B. Curtains, coverings, cords.
  C. Under Aaron's supervision.

IV. Specific Merarian directives.
  A. Service tenure established.
  B. Boards, pillars, fasteners.
  C. Priestly supervision.

V. Leadership compliance.
  A. Labor scope census.
  B. Assigned sacred labor force.

CHAPTER 5

I. Quarantine for uncleanness.
   A. Leprous separated.
   B. Defilement by the dead.
   C. The camp of God's presence.
II. Trespass guiltiness.
   A. Confession for sin.
   B. Recompense ratio.
   C. Priestly substitute.
III. Marital infidelity of a wife.
   A. Secretive.
   B. Jealousy proved or disproved.
   C. Priestly test for veracity.
   D. Guilty bears own iniquity.

CHAPTER 6

I. The separation of a Nazarite.
   A. Man or woman.
   B. No strong drink.
   C. No food from vine.
   D. No razor used.
   E. No contact with body of the dead.
II. Cleansing of defiled Nazarite.
   A. Unavoidable defilement by sudden death.
   B. Immediate razor use.
   C. Offerings presented.
      1. Time lapse.
      2. Kind and amount.
   D. Consecration time lost.
III. Nazarite separation ended.
   A. Presented at door of tabernacle.
   B. Appropriate offerings.
      1. First year perfect ram for burnt offering.
      2. First year perfect ewe for sin offering.
      3. One perfect ram for peace offering.
      4. Unleaven bread prepared for meal offering.
      5. Priest officiating.
   C. Shaved head.
   D. Burned hair.
   E. Wave offering properly performed.
      1. Nazarite identified with offering.
      2. Priest's portion.
   F. Free from separation.
   G. Vow obligation binding.
IV. Priestly blessing.
   A. Identified with Source of Blessing.
   B. Recognition of Divine Reality.
   C. Proof of Presence.
   D. Gracious giving.
   E. Protective peace.
   F. Witnessing worship.

CHAPTER 7

I. Dedicatory worship.
   A. Anointed tabernacle.
   B. Sanctified vessels.
   C. Offerings by tribes via princes.
      1. Six wagons — 1 per 2 princes.
      2. Twelve oxen — 1 per prince.
   D. Acceptance directive.
   E. Use assignments.
   F. Transportation schedule.
II. Initial altar offerings by tribes.
   A. Tribal prince led.
   B. Designated days.
      1. One silver charger, 130 shekel weight.
      2. One silver bowl, 70 shekel weight.

3. Both filled with fine flour and oil.
4. One gold spoon, 10 shekels.
5. Burnt offering.
   a. One young bullock.
   b. One lamb.
   c. One lamb of first year.
6. One kid of the goats for sin offering.
7. Peace offering.
   a. Two oxen.
   b. Five rams.
   c. Five male goats.
   d. Five lambs of the first year.

III. Conference of confirmation.
   A. Moses in tabernacle of congregation.
   B. God spoke from Mercy Seat above Ark.

CHAPTER 8

I. Lamp lighting time.
   A. High priest's responsibility.
   B. Lamps for light.
   C. Artistry of craftsmen.
   D. Made to pattern.
II. Dedicated Levites.
   A. Cleansing procedure.
      1. Sprinkling of purification.
      2. Complete shave.
      3. Laundered clothes.
   B. Full offerings of dedication.
      1. One young bullock.
      2. Meal offering, mingled with oil.
      3. One young bullock for sin offering.
   C. Before whole congregation.
   D. Identified with Israelites.
   E. Full presentation to God.
   F. Levites identified with offerings.
   G. Levites service consecration.
III. Firstborn of Israel replaced.
   A. God's ownership declared.
   B. God's verification vindicated.
IV. Obedience to directives.
   A. Service years established.
   B. Congregation acceptability in retirement.

CHAPTER 9

I. Passover's first anniversary.
   A. Sinai's shadow.
   B. Responsibility unchanged.
   C. Compliance concluded.
   D. Defilement or distance delays.
      1. One month delay.
      2. No excuse acceptable.
      3. No redemption without compliance.
   E. Provision for stranger.
      1. One formula for all.
      2. Full obedience for all.
II. Tabernacle witnessing.
   A. God's presence seen by all.
      1. A cloud by day.
      2. A pillar of fire by night.
   B. Camp duration according to the cloud.
      1. Dwelling in camp by clouds presence.

    2. Journeying as cloud is lifted.
  C. God's commands governed travels.

CHAPTER 10

I. Trumpet signals.
  A. Metal, style, number.
  B. Uses.
    1. Calling full assembly — two trumpets.
    2. Calling princes — one trumpet.
    3. Calling marching alarms.
    4. No alarms for assemblies.
    5. Alarm calls for war dangers.
      a. Witness of God's presence.
      b. Victory assured for obedience.
    6. Trumpets sound in gladness.
    7. Trumpets sound in worship.
  C. Trumpeters among the priests.
II. Cloud signals.
  A. Calendar significance.
    1. Time for complete compliance.
    2. Time to practice God's presence.
  B. Marching order established.
    1. East camps first
    2. Gershonites with tabernacle.
    3. South camps in third place.
    4. Kohathites with sanctuary.
    5. West camps in fifth place.
    6. North camps in sixth, or last place.
III. A guide's call to service.
  A. Invitation to Hobab.
  B. The promised good.
  C. Determined refusal.
  D. Earnest entreaty.
    1. Mutual helpfulness.
    2. Reciprocal blessings.
IV. Journey's pattern
  A. Led by the Ark under the cloud.
  B. Journey blessing.
  C. Camp blessing.

CHAPTER 11

I. Complaining followers.
  A. Shortsighted recipients.
  B. A fiery judgment.
  C. Borderline victims.
  D. A leader's prayer.
  E. Judgment memorial in place name.
  F. Appetites in control.
    1. Lament in memories.
    2. Lamentable loathings.
  G. A leader's lament.
    1. Displeasure.
    2. Despondency.
    3. Debility in spirit.
II. Shared responsibilities.
  A. The called-out ones.
  B. Confrontation with Deity.
  C. Proclaimed provisions.
  D. Power of all providence.
  E. Doubting leadership
  F. Shared spirit of prophesying.

NUMBERS

    1. Perturbed populous.
    2. Prayerful proposition.
III. Meat of magnanimity.
    A. Wind for wantonness.
    B. Willful wantonness displayed.
    C. A plague of judgment.
    D. A name for remembrance.

CHAPTER 12

I. Jealousy in leadership.
    A. Superficial reasoning.
    B. Egocentricity.
    C. Unrecognized honor.
    D. Didactic conference.
        1. Deity's presence.
        2. Deity's purpose.
        3. Deity's preferment.
    E. Divine justice.
II. Repentance.
    A. Acknowledged sin.
    B. Plea for release.
    C. Prayer for healing.
III. Removal.
    A. Analogy for shame.
    B. Quarantine time.
IV. Restoration.
V. Resumed journey.

CHAPTER 13

I. Spy selection.
    A. Divine directive.
    B. Tribal leaders or rulers.
    C. Comprehensive reconnaissance.
    D. Visible proof required.
II. Spy perspective.
    A. Places of inspection.
    B. Period of inspection.
III. Spy report.
    A. Adequate land.
    B. Adequate harvest possibilities.
    C. Adequate population.
        1. Worth possessing.
        2. Impossible possession.
        3. Minority report.
    F. Majority report prevails.

CHAPTER 14

I. A night of grief.
    A. The tears of a closed mind.
    B. The longing of a short vision.
    C. The brash thinking of rebel hearts.
    D. The consternation of leadership.
    E. The bravery of loyal faith.
        1. Token actions of sorrow.
        2. Reviewed assets.
        3. Proof of the *Lord's* delight.
        4. Value in possession.
    F. The reaction of blind fear.
II. Divine response.
    A. Time limitations.
    B. Spiritual blindness.
    C. Proposed judgment.
    D. Postponed fulfillment.
    E. Human reasoning.
    F. Prayer for pardon.
    G. Judgment pronounced.
        1. Reminders of rebellion.
        2. Exemption for minority.
        3. Victory for "helpless."
        4. Postponement time set.
        5. Blind majority removed.

H. Belated submission.
   I. Rebelliousness remained.
   J. Human plans fail.

CHAPTER 15 (cf. Lev. chap. 1-7)

   I. Promised land offerings by fire.
      A. Type and materials.
      B. Accouterments ratio.
      C. Personal responsibility.
         1. Indigene.
         2. Alien (stranger).
  II. Promised land sustenance offering.
      A. Heave offering.
      B. Firstfruit dough offering.
      C. Omission through ignorance offering.
      D. Perpetual requirement.
         1. By congregation
         2. By individual.
      E. Presumptuous omissions *anathema.*
 III. Wilderness Sabbath breaking.
      A. Wood gathering.
      B. Isolation ward.
      C. Judgment pronounced.
      D. Sentence executed for example.
  IV. Perpetual wardrobe reminders.
      A. Fringe borders on garments.
      B. Reminders of multiple commandments.
      C. Witnessing agency.

CHAPTER 16

   I. Presumptions of would be leaders.
      A. Dedicated family background.
      B. Gained a following.
      C. Bold claim of holiness.
      D. Misguided accusations.
  II. Humility in leadership.
      A. Submission to divine leadership.
      B. The test of sincerity.
      C. Worshipful presentation.
      D. Reviewed favorable status.
      E. Prideful ambition recognized.
 III. Rebellion to leadership.
      A. Refused command of leadership.
      B. Boastful resistance.
      C. Impossible demands.
      D. Impeccable defense.
  IV. Showdown in leadership.
      A. Rebellion presented.
      B. Congregation separated.
      C. The test time set.
      D. God's answer as proof.
      E. Congregation in full sight.
      F. Rebel censers as memorials.
   V. Murmurs against leadership.
      A. Misplaced blame.
      B. Punishment in plague.
      C. Priestly intermission.

CHAPTER 17

   I. Test of priesthood.
      A. Tribal leaders on named rods.
      B. Rods in congregational tabernacle.
      C. Time lapse.
  II. Proof of priesthood.
      A. Ample evidence of living proof.
      B. Memorial of proof.
      C. Testimony of proof.
 III. Fear of priesthood.
      A. Reprisals imagined.

B. Separation imagined.
   C. Annihilation imagined.

CHAPTER 18

I. Levitical responsibility.
   A. In sole charge of tabernacle.
   B. Priest's duties separate.
   C. Strangers separated.
   D. Personal preservation.
II. Levitical portion.
   A. In lieu of landed estates.
   B. Tithes of Israel.
   C. Tithe of tithes by priests.
   D. Meat and meal offerings.
   E. First fruits designated.
   F. Redeemed redeemable.
   G. Fidelity to prevent sin.

CHAPTER 19

I. The offering of separation.
   A. Designated victim.
   B. Congregational gift.
   C. Slain in priest's sight.
   D. Blood of separation applied.
   E. Complete destruction by fire.
   F. Ashes enriched.
   G. Uncleanness in participation in rites.
II. The water of separation.
   A. Ashes of sacrifice preserved.
   B. Contamination in collecting ashes.
   C. Perpetual ordinance of cleansing.
   D. Non-discriminatory in use.
   E. Schedule for cleansing.
   F. Stringent treatment for violators.
   G. Indictments of uncleanness.
   H. Cleansing schedule established.
      1. Applicator.
      2. Applicant.
      3. Appertainment.

CHAPTER 20

I. A desert without water.
   A. The second murmur.
      1. Repetitious.
      2. Vicarious blame.
   B. Perturbed leadership.
      1. Prostrated.
      2. Power of His presence.
   C. Divine deliverance.
II. A desert without faith.
   A. Blind complaints of congregation.
   B. Blind anger at congregation.
   C. Blind disregard for command.
   D. Blind acceptance of compassion.
   E. Blind disobedience judged.
III. A desert without neighborly fellowship.
   A. Claim of kinship.
   B. Deliverance review.
   C. Requested highway use.
   D. Passage denied.
   E. Bypassed brotherhood.
IV. A desert without joy.
   A. Judgment for rebel leadership begins.
   B. Prefuneral mortuary directives.
      1. Place.
      2. Preparation.
      3. Performance.

C. Death of Aaron.
   D. Mourning period.

CHAPTER 21

I. Pre-invasion opposition.
   A. Aftermath of spy trip.
   B. Aggression.
   C. Israel's victory.
II. Journey galls.
   A. Multiple complaints.
      1. Limited food.
      2. Long travels.
      3. Longings for comforts in serfdom.
   B. Natural judgment.
   C. Repentant Israel.
   D. Relief sans removal.
      1. Looking.
      2. Living.
   E. Travel log.
      1. Promised needs.
      2. Praise in song.
III. Travel projections.
   A. Permission requested.
   B. Permission denied in attack.
   C. Possession replaces permission.
      1. Sihon.
      2. Heshbon.
      3. Bashan.

CHAPTER 22

I. Moab murmurings.
   A. Review of invasion.
   B. Balak's blunders.
      1. Bounty for blessings.
      2. Balaam bound.
         a. Lip loyalty.
         b. Covetousness.
         c. Blindness to evil way.

II. Balaam at work.
   A. Word power prescribed.
   B. Panoramic view.

CHAPTER 23

   C. Altar approach.
   D. Worshipful claim.
   E. Limited word power.
   F. Wishful identity.
   G. Woeful rebuke.
   H. Repeated attempts.
   I. Frustration complete.

CHAPTER 24

   J. Visions of Israel's successes.
   K. Dismissal in disgrace.
      1. Blamed for failure.
      2. Misplaced blame for withheld rewards.
III. Balaam's prophecies.
   A. Open-eyed vision.
   B. Moab victimized.
   C. Edom's servitude.
   D. Amalek as example.
   E. Kenites' limited security.
   F. All aggressors victimized in turn.
IV. Balaam and Balak apart.

CHAPTER 25

I. Moab's revenge.
   A. Duo-unfaithfulness.
   B. Drastic judgment.
II. Flagrant disobedience.
   A. Disregard for neighbor's sorrow.
   B. Arrogant defiant action.
   C. Drastic retaliation.
III. Moab's victory.
   A. More subtle than Balaam's curse.

- B. Idol worshiping.
- C. Victims of punishing plague.
- D. Zealous priest rewarded.
IV. Moab's punishment.
- A. Memorial in priest's citation.
- B. Object of warfare.
- C. Princely leadership condemned.

CHAPTER 26

I. Induction and land division census.
- A. Recognition of loss by the plague.
- B. Recognition of family histories.
- C. Totals in man power.

II. Land division basis.
- A. Numerical ratio.
- B. Division by lot.
- C. Levites denied land inheritance.

III. Wilderness wanderings near completion.
- A. Rejecters removed by death.
- B. Rewards to the remainder.

CHAPTER 27

I. Patrimony plea.
- A. Daughters' desires.
  1. Merit review.
  2. Inheritance rights.
- B. Highest authority sought.

II. Patrimony schedule summarized.
- A. First example.
- B. Subsequent pattern.

III. Presaged departure.
- A. Imminent event.
- B. Planned preview of promised land.
- C. Logical consequence.
- D. The plea for a replacement.

IV. Succession in leadership.
- A. Designated.
- B. Dedicated.
- C. Devoted.
- D. Delivered (ordained).

CHAPTER 28

I. Daily offerings review.
- A. Planned schedule.
- B. Picked portions.
- C. Prescribed procedures.
  1. Recipient.
  2. Timed.

II. Sabbath offerings review.
- A. Double portions.
- B. Detailed components.
- C. Continued practice.

III. Month beginning offerings review.
- A. Increased portions.
- B. Designed delegation of constituents.
- C. Twelve performances per year.

IV. Passover offering review.
- A. Time designated.
- B. Preparation prescribed.
- C. Duo-sabbath terminus.
- D. Nationwide observance.
  1. Congregational application.
  2. Family participation.
  3. Daily schedule.

V. Firstfruits offering review.
- A. Harvest inspired.

B. Work restructions.
  C. Special connotations.
   1. Portions.
   2. Additional devotion.

CHAPTER 29

I. Seventh month solemn feasts.
  A. Calendar schedule.
   1. First day.
   2. Offerings outlined.
     a. Animal sacrifice.
     b. Meal offerings.
   3. Tenth day convocation.
     a. Dedicated observance.
     b. Labor limited.
     c. Animal sacrifice duplication.
  B. Regressive offering schedules.
   1. Each day's limitations.
   2. Uniform procedure.
   3. Stated purposes.
  C. Solemn assembly.
   1. End of special week.
   2. Special sabbath restrictions.
II. Purposeful worship.
  A. Offerings to the Lord.
  B. Sin offerings for man.
  C. Additional pattern.
  D. Continual testimony.

CHAPTER 30

I. A personal vow obligation.
  A. Man non-exempted.
  B. Woman's way out.
   1. Disallowed by father or husband.
   2. Binding in silence of father or spouse.
   3. Forgiveness for disallowance.
  C. Widows and divorcees non-exempted.
II. Indorsement obligations.
  A. Immediate indorsement in silence.
  B. Vicarious guilt in belated objection.
  C. The Lord's decrees (statutes).

CHAPTER 31

I. Judgment against Midian.
  A. Moses's final aggression.
  B. Limited conscription.
  C. The sound of battle trumpets.
II. Defeat of Midian.
  A. Midian manpower ended.
  B. Spoils of war.
   1. Women and children.
   2. Herds and flocks.
   3. Goods of value.
  C. Spoils divided.
   1. Male children rejected.
   2. Only virgins acceptable.
   3. Separation for cleansing.
     a. Cleansing by refining fire.
     b. Cleansing by water of separation.
   4. Proportionate sharing.
   5. Levitical portion selected.
     a. Army portion.
     b. Congregation portion.

NUMBERS

      6. Memorial offering to the Lord.

CHAPTER 32

I. Plea for pasture lands.
   A. Two-and-one-half tribes' request.
   B. Conquered land ready.
   C. Selfish purpose tested.
   D. Father's rebellion reviewed.

II. Pledge of support for conquest.
   A. Safety for families and flocks.
   B. Army power promised.
   C. Word integrity test basis.
      1. Blessings for compliance.
      2. Sin guiltiness for failure.

III. Possessions established.
   A. Successive leadership to judge.
   B. Division of Gilead.

CHAPTER 33

I. Log of journeyings.
   A. Time and place of departure.
   B. Station by station account.
   C. Aaron's demise.
   D. The door of opportunities.

II. Logistics for the conquest.
   A. Complete possession required.
   B. Total removal of infidelity trends.
   C. Decreed by the Lord.
   D. Proportional equitable land allotment.
   E. Warning against less than full trust.
   F. Vicarious punishment possible.

CHAPTER 34

I. Land inheritance borders.
   A. Four point limitations.
   B. "Cousins' " occupations exempted.
   C. Recognized pre-assignments.

II. Division personnel.
   A. Spiritual and administrative supervision.
   B. Tribal representatives named.

CHAPTER 35

I. Levitical land allotments.
   A. Cities for residency.
   B. Pasturing suburbs.
   C. Proportionate distributions.
   D. Six cities for refuge.
      1. A place safe from avengers.
      2. No discrimination.
      3. Both sides of Jordan River.

II. Eligibility for refuge.
   A. Murder defined.
   B. Involuntary manslaughter described.
   C. Safe refuge restrictions.
   D. Bribery outlawed.
   E. Undefiled land, a necessity.

CHAPTER 36

I. Application of daughters' inheritance law.
   A. Zelophehad as example.
   B. Safeguard for landed estates.
   C. Jubilee equalization stipulated.

II. Primogeniture protected.
   A. Tribal husbands.
   B. Faithful law observance.

DEUTERONOMY

CHAPTER 1

I. The place and time of review.
   A. East of Jordan.
   B. After forty years of wandering.
   C. After Amorite conquest.

II. Introduction and summary of review.
   A. End results finally.
   B. Command from Horeb's heights.
   C. Conquest presented.
   D. Delegated responsibility.
   E. Parenthetic blessing.
   F. Communal agreement.
   G. Judges' responsibilities.

III. Border position in review.
   A. Frontier of camp site.
   B. Frontier of faith.
   C. Frontier in caution.
      1. Reconnaissance for strategy?
      2. Stalling, a blanket for fear.
   D. Repetitious rebellion.
   E. Deaf ears to courage appeal.

IV. Border rebellion judgment reviewed.
   A. Consigned to failure.
   B. Promised success for frailties.
      1. Children conquerors in prospect.
      2. Two adult exemptions.
   C. Rebellion against judgment.
   D. Strengthless aggression.
   E. A camp of tears.

CHAPTER 2

I. The circle march.
   A. Return from Kadesh-barnea.
   B. Round and round Mount Seir.

II. The brethren by-pass march.
   A. Esau exempt from exploitation.
   B. Lot's descendants spared aggression.
   C. Examples of conquest reviewed.
   D. Thirty-eight year reminders.

III. The pre-conquest march (vv. 16, 24).
   A. After death of all rebel fathers.
   B. Primal possessions possible.
   C. Pattern of fear established.
   D. Polite plea.

E. Requests rejected.
F. Review of rewarding reactions.
G. Annihilation for antagonists.

CHAPTER 3

I. The fall of first, and "last," giant.
   A. Repetition of first victory.
   B. Heathen removal.
   C. Victors' spoils.
      1. Personal property.
      2. Landed possessions.
      3. Land allotments.
II. Pledge reminders.
   A. Established family safety.
   B. Promised conquest aid for brethren.
   C. Leadership succession.
   D. Promised victories.
   E. Request for reprieve denied.

CHAPTER 4

I. The commandment in-reach.
   A. Inward acceptance
   B. No augments nor deletions.
   C. Force of examples.
      1. Victories achieved under auspices.
      2. Life preserved in obediences.
      3. Mission possibilities.
   D. Exclusive privileges.
   E. Power of remembrances.
      1. Initial declaration at Horeb.
      2. Permanency in stone and hearts.
II. The commandment outreach.
   A. Obligation to teach commandments.
   B. Singular devotions.
      1. No idol worship.
      2. No nature worship.
   C. Living witnesses.
   D. Blameworthy justice.
   E. Progenitor obligation.
   F. Warning for disobedient.
      1. Aroused jealous God.
      2. Forced idolatry as punishment.
   G. Hope for repentant.
III. The commandment in active practice.
   A. Cities of refuge designated.
   B. Possessions of two-and-one-half tribes.

CHAPTER 5

I. Scribal law promulgator review.
   A. Recall of background.
   B. Personnel involvement.
   C. Deity's pre-eminence.
   D. Mediator's role.
II. The Law restated.
   A. Exact copy.
   B. Penalties intact.
   C. Recognized authority.
III. Human frailties.
   A. Fear of close fellowship.
   B. Lack of precedent.
   C. *Days man* demanded (Job 9:33).
   D. Promised compliance.
   E. God's sanction.
   F. Didactic responsibility.
   G. Longevity and prosperity contingency.

CHAPTER 6

I. Reminding forecast.
   A. Law review for pattern setting.
   B. A didactic inheritance.
   C. One road to progress.
II. Pervading motivation.
   A. *Agape* in force.
   B. Heart inventory.
   C. Pedagogical precept and practice.
   D. Living lines of communication.
   E. Purpose for prosperous possession.
   F. Warning for wandering wants.
III. Sternness against stubbornness.
   A. Danger in selfish tests.
   B. Complete separation required.
   C. Concise, concrete compliance.
   D. Conditional continuance.

CHAPTER 7

I. Warning against pseudo-mercy.
   A. No fraternizing.
   B. No intermarriages.
   C. Complete removal of false worship.
II. Divine purpose reviewed.
   A. Special predestination.
   B. The Lord's illogical choice.
   C. The integrity of Deity.
   D. The proof of Deity.
III. Dedication to Deity's Design
   A. Obedience required.
   B. Blessings in conquest.
      1. Prosperity.
      2. Health.
      3. Victory.
      4. Courage assured.

   C. Strengthening recall.
   D. Progressive conquest.
   E. Complete separation reiterated.

CHAPTER 8

I. Review of the past.
   A. Forty years of Divine care.
   B. Didactic purpose.
   C. Feast and famine.
   D. Miraculous provisions.
   E. Lessons in chastisements.
II. Responsibilities for the present.
   A. Prospectus of the open door.
   B. Dangers in abundant prosperity.
   C. Necessity for gratitude.
III. Reminders in prognostication.
   A. Recall past blessings.
   B. Forestall arrogant pride.
   C. Remember source of wealth.
   D. No impunity for disobedience.

CHAPTER 9

I. Threshold reminders.
   A. Zero hour.
   B. Gigantic opposition.
   C. Recognition of source of power.
   D. Remembering cause for victory.
II. Rebellious record recall.
   A. Day of departure pattern.
   B. Shortsighted patience.
   C. Regal rejection.
   D. Rival in regency.
   E. Repentant request.
      1. Funneled fulminations.

DEUTERONOMY

2. Covenant conditions.

CHAPTER 10
I. The rewrite.
   A. Preparation responsibility.
   B. Provision for safe deposit.
   C. Perfected enterprise.
II. Projected review.
   A. Place names.
   B. Personnel separation.
   C. Protected heritage.
   D. Prayer for providence.
   E. Prescribed prescription.
III. Personal prosperity of spirit.
   A. Recognize requirements.
   B. Orientated to ownership of the world.
   C. Diligent demeanor.
   D. Love is the long view.
      1. Present, past, prospect.
      2. Covenant conformity.

CHAPTER 11
I. Obligations in oblations.
   A. Empirical recall.
      1. Egyptian experiences.
      2. Wilderness wanderings.
   B. Rational reasons.
      1. Laminated land.
      2. Constrained composure.
   C. Perpetual propensities.
II. Prosperity prognosticated.
   A. Complete commitment.
   B. Dedicated didacticism.
   C. Prolonged providence.
   D. Selective choices.
   E. Mounts of missions.
   F. Open opportunities.

CHAPTER 12
I. Judgment jurisdictions.
   A. Domain of doing.
   B. Worship worthily.
   C. Place for piety (vv. 5, 11, 14).
   D. Prohibited personal choices.
   E. Rejoicing religion.
   F. Magnanimity to ministering tribe (vv. 12, 18-19).
II. Nonrestricted eating.
   A. Under law schedule.
   B. No personal rejection.
   C. Blood always excluded.
   D. Specified place.
   E. Danger in success and affluence.
III. The power of testimony.
   A. Continued well-being.
   B. God's presence attested.
   C. Warning temptations.
   D. Meticulous maintenance.

CHAPTER 13
I. False dreamer-prophet.
   A. Possible fulfillment.
   B. No verification in fulfillment.
   C. Right of choice strengthened.
   D. Removal of perversity.
II. False family.
   A. No distinction in relationships.
   B. Adamant resistance demanded.
   C. No leniency allowed.
III. False community.
   A. Rumor route regarded.
   B. Source check for newsworthiness.

C. No quarter granted for offenders.
D. No sanctity in spoils.
E. Proof of fidelity.

CHAPTER 14

I. Peculiar people.
   A. No facial disfiguration.
   B. Diet restrictions reviewed.
   C. Determining demerits.
   D. Habitats, physical features, habits.
II. Peculiar polity.
   A. Selected source for meat.
   B. Selected cooking practices.
   C. Stewardship regularity.
   D. Stewardship in proof of piety.
   E. Distances regulations.
   F. Convenience allowance.
   G. Rejoice in witnessing.
   H. Benevolence in action.

CHAPTER 15

I. Egalitarian sociology.
   A. Benevolence vs. selfishness.
   B. Non-familial exemptions.
   C. Improbable exemptions (vv. 5, 11n Mark 14:7).
   D. Compliant Croesuses.
      1. Lenders, not borrowers.
      2. Rulers, not the ruled.
II. Welfare practices.
   A. Compassion at work.
   B. No time consciousness.
   C. Release benefits.
   D. No coercion.
   E. Marked to serve by choice.
III. Meat dining measures.
   A. Firstlings of herds and flocks.

B. Family affair.
C. Perfect specimen.
D. No personal exemptions.
E. Usual blood exclusion.

CHAPTER 16

I. Passover preview.
   A. Memorial measures.
   B. Reduplicated requirements.
   C. Place provisions.
   D. Persons participating.
   E. Reminiscence respects.
   F. Time tenure.
II. Feasts' fulfillments.
   A. All adult males.
   B. Tercet termini.
   C. Stewardship supplements.
III. Judicial jurisdictions.
   A. Convenient courts.
   B. Banned bribery.
   C. Circumscribed conduct.
IV. Altar alinements.
   A. No trees.
   B. No images.

CHAPTER 17

I. Sacrosanct sacrifices.
   A. Perfect specimens.
   B. Abandoned abominations.
II. Recreant rejection.
   A. Reliable report.
      1. Required reporters.
      2. Stony summation.
   B. Appeal application.
   C. Decree determined.
   D. Exact executions.
   E. No pampered presumption.
III. Regal royalty.
   A. Designated by Deity.
   B. Department delineated.

DEUTERONOMY

C. Didactic demands.
D. Longevity in loyalty.

CHAPTER 18

I. Patrimony of Levites.
   A. The Lord as their inheritance.
   B. Shared offering portions.
   C. Varied service places.
II. Necromancy nullified.
   A. Such learning off limits.
   B. Human sacrifice shunned.
   C. Separated from Canaanitish patterns.
III. Prophetic patrimony.
   A. Replacement provided.
   B. Befitting pattern.
   C. Commensurate with demands.
   D. Limits of messages.
   E. Proof for presumption.

CHAPTER 19

Cities of refuge.
   A. Equitable distribution.
   B. Safe for involuntary manslaughter.
   C. Avenger restricted.
   D. City number increased as needed.
   E. Designed to spare the innocent.
II. No refuge for murderer.
   A. Obligatory surrender of guilty.
   B. No provision for pity.
III. Property rights inviolate.
   A. Permanent landmarks.
   B. Minimum witness requirement.
   C. Proof for veracity.

D. No impunity for schemers.
E. The power of example.

CHAPTER 20

I. Impunity for brainwashing.
   A. Enemy armament inadequate.
   B. Priestly preparation.
II. Deferment provisions.
   A. Housing restrictions (v. 5).
   B. Occupational deprivations.
   C. Marital frustrations.
   D. Examples of fainthearted.
III. Peace overtures.
   A. Submission or subjection.
      1. Tributaries in submission.
      2. Annihilation in subjection.
   B. Legitimate spoils.
IV. Battle strategies.
   A. Varied by proximity.
   B. No allowance for reversions.
   C. Conservative concepts.
      1. Forestry exemptions.
      2. Forestry uses.

CHAPTER 21

I. Coroner's report.
   A. Manslaughter of unknown cause.
   B. Habitation in proximity selected.
   C. Offering for innocency.
   D. Priestly court of jurisprudence.
   E. Accepted affidavits.
II. Spoils of war prize.
   A. Worthy aspiration.
   B. Cleansing practice.

C. Reasonable mourning period.
D. Marital consummation.
E. Freedom in separation.
 1. Way of choice.
 2. Exemption from slave status.
III. Primogenture pattern.
 A. Jacobean experience.
 B. Actual firstborn rights.
IV. Parental discipline.
 A. Stubborn rebellion.
 B. Inadequate parental control.
 C. Responsibility for report.
 D. Community obligation.
V. Capital punishment.
 A. Proper condemnation.
 B. Execution by hanging.
  1. Attendant curse association.
  2. Removal before sundown.
 C. National integrity.

CHAPTER 22

I. Lost and found department.
 A. Straying livestock.
 B. Return or safe-keeping.
 C. Personal property.
 D. Helpful service.
II. Eithical implications.
 A. Public wardrobe (vv. 5, 11-12).
 B. Wild game.
 C. Safety measures in construction.
 D. Horticulture practice.
 E. Soil husbandry.
III. Marital ethics.
 A. Selfish slander proof.
 B. Punishment for the guilty.
 C. Promiscuity condemnatory.
 D. Offender's responsibility.
  1. Face guilt.
  2. Legal rectification.
 E. Domestic integrity.

CHAPTER 23

I. Exclusions from worship participation.
 A. Physical mutilations.
 B. Illegitimacy.
 C. Alien enemies.
  1. Denied sustenance for money.
  2. Hired Balaam to curse.
 D. Brotherhood limits.
  1. Former relationship.
  2. Former location.
  3. Acceptability provisions.
 E. Separation in war.
II. Cleansing procedures.
 A. Isolation period.
 B. Sanitation safeguards.
 C. Fit camp for God's presence.
III. Personal worth.
 A. Escaped serfs honored.
 B. Womanhood morality above reproach.
 C. Source of money offering limited.
 D. Business integrity defined.
IV. Sanctity of vows.
 A. Spoken vow validity.
 B. Highest authority requirement.
 C. Reneged guiltiness.
 D. Freewill obligations.

DEUTERONOMY

V. Gleaning limitations.
   A. Personal momentary needs only.
   B. Harvest restricted.

CHAPTER 24
I. Marital practices.
   A. Dissatisfaction by uncleanness.
   B. Divorce provisions.
   C. Remarrying limitations.
   D. Marital exemptions.
II. Property rights.
   A. Loan security liabilities.
   B. Slavery under severe penalties.
   C. Collateral removed from force.
III. Leprosy isolation.
   A. Health protection.
   B. Example patterns.
IV. Personal rights.
   A. Hired help.
   B. Punctual payments.
   C. Equitable judgment demanded.
   D. Remember the past.
   E. Gleaning for welfare needs.
   F. Effective witnessing.

CHAPTER 25
I. Courts in action.
   A. Civil controversies.
   B. Correct decisions.
   C. Correct execution of sentence.
   D. Humane practices.
II. Inheritance corrections.
   A. Heirless brother consideration.
   B. Widow rights.
   C. Established record.
III. Immodest womanhood.
   A. Endangered husband.
   B. Impropriety.
   C. Severity in punishment.
IV. Measurement standards.
   A. Justice in commerce.
   B. Longevity assured.
   C. Separated from unrighteousness.
V. Amalekitish pattern.
   A. Opposition to Israel.
   B. Remembered retribution.

CHAPTER 26
I. Possession gratitude.
   A. Firstfruit offering.
   B. Shared bounty.
   C. Selected place.
   D. Presented to priests.
   E. Remembrances.
   F. Providential abundance.
II. Stewardship of tithes.
   A. The year of the tithe.
   B. The welfare application.
   C. Compliance complete.
   D. Prayer of dedication.
III. Peculiar testimony.
   A. Timely commandments.
   B. Avowed devotions.
   C. Position of purpose.

CHAPTER 27
I. The time for full commitment.
   A. Wanderings behind.
   B. Threshold before.
   C. Memorial monuments.
   D. Permanent commandment copy.
   E. Whole stone altar.
II. Ownership established.
   A. Are become people of God.

B. Obedience required.
C. Emphasis on choice ritual.
  1. Blessings.
  2. Curses.
D. Tribal pronouncement designated.
E. Curse review.
  1. Socio-religious.
  2. Personal endorsement.

CHAPTER 28

I. Blessings schedule.
  A. Choice of action.
  B. Overall picture.
    1. Location for avocations.
    2. Posterity assured.
    3. Prosperity, natural result.
    4. Provision bounty.
    5. Proficiency in defense.
    6. Piety honored.
  C. Overtures for witnessing.
    1. Obedience for manifold purpose.
    2. Proof of covenant.
    3. Drawing power of providence.
    4. Financial position.
II. But curses for apostasy.
  A. Choice paramount.
  B. Magnitude in scope.
    1. Health hazards added.
    2. Weather hazards disproportionate.
    3. Slavery for posterity.
    4. Exile possibilities.
    5. General economic reverses.
    6. Cannibalism in extremities.
  C. Witnessing through adversities.
    1. Purpose of punishment.
    2. Projection of punishment.
    3. Perturbation in punishment.

CHAPTER 29

I. Covenant renewal time.
  A. Law review ended.
  B. Blessing vs. curse schedule known.
  C. Reviewed historical events.
    1. Journey.
    2. Providence.
    3. Presaging conquest pattern.
  D. Continued condonation conditional.
  E. Complete commitment.
    1. Leadership.
    2. Families.
    3. Servants.
    4. Absentees.
  F. Recall evils of idolatry.
    1. Strength against temptations.
    2. Warning against personal impunity.
    3. Recognition of separation from evil.
  G. Covenant violators.

CHAPTER 30

I. Foreign missions.
  A. Living testimony in captivity.
  B. Promised restoration.
  C. Renewed covenant relationship.

        D. Innate separation.
        E. Transfer of punitiveness.
        F. No surcease of obedience.
  II. Open-door policy.
        A. Non-secretive code.
        B. All tangibility.
        C. Proximity.
        D. Twofold duo-choice.
        E. Explicit warnings.
        F. Deity's dependability.

CHAPTER 31

  I. A leader's farewell.
        A. Directive limitation.
        B. Expression of confidence.
        C. Plea for courage.
  II. A mantle passed on.
        A. New leadership.
        B. Public pronouncement.
        C. Reason for hope.
  III. Recorder's obligation.
        A. Accurate records.
        B. Safety depository (vv. 9, 25, 26).
        C. Review schedule.
            1. Regular.
            2. Congregation involvement.
            3. Didactic purpose.
  IV. Deity's dismissal
        A. Declaration of demarcation.
        B. Delivered charge.
        C. Dedication demeanor.
        D. Deflections delineated.
  V. Oral presentation of farewell address.
        A. Assembly call.
        B. Multiple endorsement.
        C. Apostasy forecast.

CHAPTER 32

  I. Preamble.
        A. Refreshing remembrance.
        B. Grandiose glory.
        C. Refulgent foundation.
        D. Reminder of God's fatherhood.
        E. Graphic concern.
  II. Rebellious rebuked.
        A. Exaggerated ego.
        B. Infidelity pattern.
            1. Forgetfulness.
            2. Idolatry.
            3. Indifference.
            4. Double rejection.
        C. Multiple fire complex.
            1. Fires of anger.
            2. Fires of punishment.
            3. Fires of persecutions.
            4. Fires of privation.
            5. Fires of rejection.
                a. Captivity.
                b. Spiritual ignorance.
                c. Withdrawn help.
                d. Pride of conquerors.
                e. Lack of real wisdom.
        D. Following pattern of Sodom.
        E. Powerless false gods.
        F. Vengeance in reverse.
  III. Appeal for permanence.
        A. Active participation required.
        B. Deeper than oral assent.
        C. Personal profit.
  IV. Preamble to departure.
        A. Preparation for demise.
        B. Review of reason for penalty.
        C. One look only.

CHAPTER 33

I. Blessing preamble.
   A. Moses's final word.
   B. Deity's personality.
      1. Presence.
      2. Shekinah glory.
      3. Purifying law.
      4. Magnanimous love.
   C. Adequate spokesman.
II. Tribal distinctions.
   A. Reuben.
      1. Longevity.
      2. Populous progeny.
   B. Judah.
      1. Voice of leadership.
      2. Restoration.
      3. Sufficient strength.
      4. Safe from enemy.
   C. Levi.
      1. Signs of dedication.
      2. Evidence of victory.
      3. Stronger than family ties.
      4. Example of obedience.
      5. Pedagogs for piety.
      6. Worship patterns.
      7. Divine providence.
   D. Benjamin.
      1. Loyal devotion.
      2. Divine protection.
      3. Undergirded.
   E. Joseph.
      1. Landed possessions blessed.
      2. Nature's favorable responses.
      3. Bountiful harvests.
      4. Mineral resources.
      5. Personal aggrandizement.
      6. United strength.
   F. Zebulun and Issachar.
      1. Progression.
      2. Domestic security.
      3. Worship provisions.
      4. Commercial advancement.
   G. Gad.
      1. Vicarious blessing.
      2. Latent ability.
      3. Equitable judgments.
   H. Dan.
      1. Strength.
      2. Aggression.
   I. Naphtali.
      1. Satisfaction in favors.
      2. Full blessings.
      3. Expanse in possession.
   J. Asher.
      1. Family expanse.
      2. Fellowship with brethren.
      3. Well-being ascribed.
      4. Expansion strength.
III. Excellency of Deity.
   A. Pervading power.
   B. Everlasting strength.
   C. Sustaining support.
   D. Safe assurance.
   E. Sustenance a surety.
   F. Undergirding utterences.
   G. Shield and sword sufficiency.

CHAPTER 34

I. Departure in action.
   A. Mount ascension by command.
   B. One long look.
   C. God's appraisal.
   C. Death, burial, and secrecy.
   E. Epitomized biography.
      1. Longevity.
      2. Preservation of natural strength.

3. Standard mourning period.
4. Exclusive leadership (vv. 10-12).

II. Successor in command.
   A. Spirit endowed, endued.
   B. Recognized priority.

JOSHUA

CHAPTER 1
I. Introduction to the task.
   A. Voice of authority.
   B. Recognized status.
   C. One way progress ahead.
   D. Victory ahead by application.
   E. Need for courage.
   F. Obedience, a must.
   G. Adherence to the Book.
   H. Hope in compliance.
II. Preparation for campaign (v. 10).
   A. Rations in preparation.
   B. D-Day determined.
   C. Reminder to tribes in possession.
   D. Full enjoyment contingencies.
   E. Renewed pledges.
   F. Capital punishment for deviates.

CHAPTER 2
I. Threefold reconnaissance.
   A. Fortification of land-cities.
   B. Fortification in defenders' spirits.
   C. Fortification in invaders' hearts.
II. CIA report.
   A. Presence known.
   B. Place of concealment surmised.

III. Filial bargaining.
   A. False trial tactics.
   B. Confessed defenseless.
   C. Life-for-a-life bargain.
   D. Escape strategy.
   E. Sign for exemption.
   F. Provision for vow termination.
IV. Encouraging report.
   A. Victory assured.
   B. Defenders with will to resist.

CHAPTER 3
I. Invasion in preparation.
   A. Camp by east side of Jordan.
   B. Marching position procedure.
   C. A new way identified.
II. Invasion in progress.
   A. Priests bearing Ark set signal.
   B. Established leadership.
   C. Fixed position of the Ark.
   D. Sign of complete conquest.
   E. Tribal emissaries for testimony.
   F. Flooded Jordan divided.
   G. Dry-shod crossing.

CHAPTER 4
I. Tribal emissaries at work.

A. Memorial stones from Jordan.
   B. Memorial site.
   C. Stones of testimony.
      1. Campsite west of Jordan.
      2. Site of priests' stance in Jordan.
II. Completed crossing of Jordan.
   A. Nine-and-a-half tribes complete.
   B. All armed men.
   C. Priests and the Ark.
   D. Jordan waters back in course.
   E. Didactic testimony of crossing.

CHAPTER 5

I. Favorable newscast.
   A. Miraculous crossing of Jordan known.
   B. Will to resist in Canaanites
II. Full return to covenant requirement.
   A. Barriers of pilgrimage removed.
      1. Death of circumcised rebels.
      2. Travel hazards past.
   B. National sign of separation.
   C. Signal of removal of Egyptian influence.
   D. Passover observance.
III. Dietary change.
   A. Stored harvest available.
   B. Manna unavailable.
   C. Land production continued source.
IV. Alert leadership.

   A. Unknown soldier ready for action.
   B. Brave encounter.
   C. Direct question.
   D. Declaration of duties.
   E. Sacred site of meeting.
   F. Worship in humility.

CHAPTER 6

I. Attack strategy outlined.
   A. Victory assured in compliance.
   B. Seven day plan.
      1. Six voiceless marches — one per day.
      2. Seventh day with seven encirclements.
      3. Ram's horn trumpet blast.
      4. Loud shout of marchers.
      5. City walls collapse.
II. Attack plan in action.
   A. Army leading.
   B. Trumpeters in second position.
   C. Priests with Ark followed trumpeters.
   D. Congregation followed Ark.
   E. Six-day pattern followed.
   F. Conquest on schedule.
      1. Seven times around Jericho.
      2. Trumpet blast.
      3. Great shout.
      4. Crumbling walls flattened.
   G. Dedicated spoils.
      1. Metalic spoils for God.

JOSHUA

    2. No life spared except as vowed.
       a. Rahab.
       b. Rahab's kin in her house.
    3. City burned.
    4. Curse on selfish spoils.
III. City site under curse.
   A. No blessing for any rebuilder.
   B. Laboriously rebuilt only with handicaps.
   C. Victory outreach.

CHAPTER 7

I. Curse of covetousness.
   A. Selfishness.
   B. Violation of divine command.
   C. National suffering.
II. Assumed guiltlessness.
   A. Future conquest plans.
   B. CIA report requested.
   C. Underestimated task.
   D. Unprecedented failure.
   E. Misplaced blame.
III. Sin in the camp.
   A. Cause of failure revealed.
   B. Third degree investigation.
   C. Confession forthcoming.
   D. Evidence produced.
   E. National justice.
     1. Glory reserved for God.
     2. National execution.

CHAPTER 8

I. Battle courage.
   A. Dismissal of fear.
   B. Full armed might.
   C. Rights to spoils.
   D. Battle plans.
II. Battle council.
   A. Delegated responsibilities.
   B. Strategic deployment.
   C. Plan of action.
   D. Plan implementation.
III. Battle action.
   A. Trap bait.
   B. Effective allurement.
   C. Empty city in manpower.
   D. Second phase signal.
   E. Perseverance in action.
IV. Battle victory.
   A. Spoils claimed.
   B. Example execution.
   C. Hanging formula followed.
   D. Approved altar stones.
   E. Acceptable worship.
   F. Law review.
   G. All personnel in worship.
   H. Blessings — curses antiphony.
   I. Fulfillment of Moses' command.

CHAPTER 9

I. Axis for defense.
   A. War hysteria.
   B. Victory reports.
   C. Partial alliance.
   D. Gideon's capitulation.
     1. Preservation strategy.
     2. Subterfuge.
II. Egoism supreme.
   A. Princes sans prayer.
   B. Blind belief.
   C. Legal vows.
III. Rude awakening.
   A. Deception revealed.
   B. Popular denunciation.
   C. Face-saving serfdom.

CHAPTER 10

I. Axis for defense.
  A. Canaanite conclave.
  B. Alarming war news.
  C. Gibeonites as quislings.
II. Agony of fear.
  A. Call to new masters.
  B. Real danger.
III. Assault defense.
  A. Promised victory.
  B. Nighttime advance.
  C. Fleeing enemies.
  D. Meteorological bombardment.
  E. The Long Day.
  F. A prison of a cave refuge.
  G. Army victory.
  H. Enemy leadership execution.
  I. A tomb of prison and refuge.
IV. Pattern of conquest continued.
  A. Jericho style of destruction.
  B. From city to city.
  C. Return to base camp.

CHAPTER 11

I. A second axis opposition.
  A. False hope in numbers.
  B. Divine-backed victory promise.
  C. Complete military victory.
    1. Armies annihilated.
    2. Armaments destroyed.
    3. Cities preserved or burned.
    4. Fulfilled command to Moses.
II. Land conquest.
  A. Topographical expanse.
  B. Extended time.
  C. One pattern exception.
  D. Deity directed.
  E. Limited giant exemptions.
  F. A rest from war.

CHAPTER 12

I. Conquest review.
  A. East of Jordan.
    1. Nations defeated.
    2. Land exemptions.
    3. Land allotment.
  B. West of Jordan.
    1. Extent of domain.
    2. Previous owners.
    3. Specified allotment.
II. Roster of conquered kings.
  A. City matched with king.
  B. Number of kings per city.
  C. Sum complete.

CHAPTER 13

I. Physical limitations.
  A. Man's age.
  B. Man's landed boundaries.
  C. Man's historic time.
II. Land division in prospect.
  A. Victory yet to be.
  B. Land limits specified.
  C. Joshua's responsibility.
III. Practice east of Jordan.
  A. Tribal designations.
  B. Moses endorsed.
  C. Levi exempted.
  D. Adequate inheritance.

CHAPTER 14

I. Land division prospect.
  A. Leadership personnel.
  B. Division by lot.
  C. A command via Moses.
    1. Partially completed.

2. Full compliance ahead.
   3. Levitical cities.
   4. Teaching purpose.
II. Ambitious request.
   A. Caleb remembers.
      1. Promise for fidelity.
      2. Fulfillment time present.
   B. Physical strength present.
   C. Difficult task demanded.
   D. Caleb's Mount Hebron.
      1. Past glories.
      2. New ownership.

CHAPTER 15

I. Land division projection.
   A. Tribal borders outlined.
      1. Judah west of Jordan.
      2. Caleb's conquest iterated.
      3. Family patriarch strategy.
      4. Splinter from family tree.
   B. Annihilate or amalgamate.

CHAPTER 16

II. Joseph in second spot.
   A. Two-pronged allocation.
      1. Half-tribe of Manasseh.
      2. Ephraim.
   B. Ephraim's borders.
   C. Mingled with Manasseh.
   D. Subjected captives to tribute.
   E. Manesseh west of Jordan.
      1. Family names.
      2. Family locations.
      3. Daughters equal as sons.
   F. Overlapping tribal cities.
   G. Land holdings as to strength.
   H. Conquer or subject to tribute.
   I. Strength to conquer needs.

CHAPTER 18

I. Tabernacle in land of promise.
   A. Fixed place of worship.
   B. Land conquest contained.
   C. Land allotment incomplete.
II. The call for fulfillment.
   A. Indifference rules.
   B. Survey committee.
   C. Equitable assignments planned.
   D. Survey report.
   E. Divisions assigned.
      1. Benjamin in land and cities, east of Judah.
      2. Simeon, south of Judah (chap. 19).
      3. Zebulum in cities and villages, north of Carmel.
      4. Issachar in sixteen cities, south of Zebulum.
      5. Asher in twenty-two cities, north of Zebulum.
      6. Naphtali in nineteen cities, east of Asher.
      7. Dan in cities and villages, extreme north.
III. Joshua's signal honor.
   A. Special city.
   B. Response to request.
   C. Climax of land divisions.

CHAPTER 20

I. Plea for refuge cities.
   A. Command implemented.
   B. Necessity iterated.
   C. Schedule for use restated.
II. Places for refuge.
   A. Kedesh, Shechem, Kirjath-arba, west of Jordan.
   B. Bezer, Ramoth, Golan, east of Jordan.
   C. Universal use.

CHAPTER 21

I. Levites remembered.
   A. Reminding request.
   B. Response to request.
   C. Cities and suburbs designated.
   D. Equitable tribal distribution.
   E. Forty-eight cities to Levites.
II. Summary of conquest.
   A. Promised land as pledged.
   B. Complete dominion.
   C. Deity's covenant verified.

CHAPTER 22

I. Discharged army.
   A. Two-and-a-half tribes released.
   B. Obligations fulfilled.
   C. Parting counsel.
   D. Share in spoils for all.
   E. Home again.
   F. The altar by Jordan.
II. Ruinous rumor.
   A. Spurious altar.
   B. Army of vengeance.
   C. Embassy of investigation.
III. Ruined rumor.
   A. Plausible explanation.
   B. Brotherhood safeguard.
   C. Test of sincerity.
   D. Proof of integrity.
   E. Dedication to one altar.
III. Brotherhood restored.
   A. Explanation accepted.
   B. Mutual blessings conferred.
   C. Witness altar established.

CHAPTER 23

I. Preamble to farewell.
   A. Assembly of leadership.
   B. Review of achievements.
      1. Championed by their God.
      2. Conquest of land.
      3. Confirmation in possession.
II. Conditioned future conquests.
   A. Obedience, a must.
   B. Failure in unfaithfulness.
   C. Entrapment in equivocation.
   D. The abiding choice of two ways.
   E. Punishment for idolatry sure and quick.

CHAPTER 24

I. Farewell assemblage.
   A. Full congregation and leaders.
   B. Abraham's example.
   C. Early deeds of trust.
   D. Brief log of logistics.
   E. Unmerited possession.
II. Dedication renewal.
   A. Requirements emphasized.
      1. Sincerity.
      2. Separation.
      3. Service.

- B. Freedom of choice remains.
- C. Power of example.
- D. Congregation commitment.
- E. Cognizance of conquest aids.
- F. Challenge of refutation.
- G. Counting the cost.
- H. Covenant confirmed.
- I. Sanctity stone at Shechem.

III. Leadership laid to rest.
- A. Joshua's death and interment.
- B. Joseph's bones interred.
- C. Eleazar died and was buried.

JUDGES

CHAPTER 1

I. Conquest plan projections.
  - A. Prayer for guidance.
  - B. Aggression directed.
  - C. Reciprocity in advance.
  - D. Victory provided.
  - E. Vengeance in kind.
  - F. Increased spoils for victor.
    1. Achash as wife.
    2. Well-watered heritage.
  - G. Kenite withdrawal.

II. Conquest plan constricted.
  - A. Judah failed in valley.
  - B. Benjamin assimilating.
  - C. Joseph exempting a quisling.
  - D. Manasseh accepting tribute.
  - E. Ephraim accepting Canaanites.
  - F. Zebulum making tributaries.
  - G. Asher dwelling among Canaanites.
  - H. Naphtali becoming tribute collectors.
  - I. Dan fleeing to mountains.

CHAPTER 2

III. Conquest plans questioned.
  - A. Power of everlasting covenant.
  - B. Power failure cause?
  - C. Broken commandments.
  - D. Duo-purpose of Canaanite remnant.
  - E. Tears of remorse.
  - F. Re-run of Joshua's farewell.
  - G. Elders in power.
  - H. Progenitors' failure.

IV. Evil road ahead.
  - A. Baalim route followed.
  - B. Idols near at hand.
  - C. Deity's ire provoked.
  - D. Spoilers become spoils.
  - E. Enmity with God reciprocal.

V. Road of return.
  - A. Repentance or remorse?
  - B. Obstinate people.
  - C. Short reform.
  - D. Repeated deliverance.
  - E. Deliverer's death as signal for deflection.

VI. Revised conquest plan.
   A. People set pattern.
   B. Limited conquest continued.
   C. Test power of residue.
   D. God vindicated.

CHAPTER 3
I. Remnant strategy.
   A. Teach self-defense.
   B. Proof of fidelity.
   C. Philistines, Phoenicians, Hivites of Lebanon.
II. Remnant false teachers.
   A. Intermarriage.
   B. Idolatry.
   C. Rejection.
   D. Subjection.
   E. Anguish in serfdom.
   F. Delivered by Othniel.
   G. Equitable judge.
   H. Forty years of rest.
III. Pattern repeated.
   A. Death of delivering judge.
   B. Evil trailblazers.
   C. Moab conquers sans Balaam.
      1. Allied with Ammon and Amalek.
      2. Eighteen years of tribute.
   D. Ingenious left-handed deliverer.
      1. Preparedness.
      2. Subtleness.
      3. Craftiness.
      4. Delayed discovery.
   E. Rally call to meet enemy.
   F. Eighty years of rest.
   G. Shamgar against Philistia.

CHAPTER 4
I. Another wrong road.
   A. Sparked by death of Judge Ehud.
   B. Oppression by Jabin's Sisera.
   C. Resulting cry of anguish.
II. Palm tree judge.
   A. Deborah, wife of Lapidoth.
   B. Itinerate case load.
   C. Leader induction.
      1. Barak called to service.
      2. Demanded moral support.
      3. Victory, but vicarious glory.
   D. The call to arms.
   E. Battle lines drawn.
   F. Sisera on the run.
      1. Fled on foot.
      2. Presumption of friendship.
      3. Overtures of Moses' in-laws.
      4. Request for falsehood.
      5. Overconfidence.
   G. Nailed down.
   H. Jabin subdued.

CHAPTER 5
I. A song of praise.
   A. Source of avenging pow
   B. Willing followers.
   C. Regal audience.
   D. God's presence recognize
   E. Desolation without Go
II. A song of leadership.
   A. Answered call to serve.
   B. Breach of fidelity flagrant.

JUDGES

    C. Lack of armament noted.
    D. Civic responsibility.
    E. Worship remembrances.
III. A song of deliverance.
    A. Responding leadership.
    B. Mustering call to arms.
    C. Multiple talents.
    D. Heart-searchings, decisions.
    E. Alibis sought.
    F. Manifold victories.
        1. River fords.
        2. Land passages.
        3. Isolated footmen.
        4. Brave womanhood.
IV. The song of false hope.
    A. Delayed "victor's" return.
    B. Hopeful courtiers.
    C. Presumptuous spoils.
V. Forty fruitful years.
    A. Prayer for complete victory.
    B. Prayer for loyalty.

CHAPTER 6

I. Another deflection.
    A. Seven years of Midian dominion.
        1. Cave dwellers now.
        2. Appropriated harvests.
        3. Midian allies.
        4. Deep poverty prevails.
    B. A cry of remorse.
    C. Prophetic probings.
        1. Poignant postview.
        2. Burrowing blame.
II. Prelude to plentitude.
    A. Angel under the oak.
    B. Careful thrasher.
    C. Greeting of courage.
    D. Skeptical response.
    E. Valiant victory predicted.
    F. Groping mind.
    G. Hospitality.
    H. Phenomenal experience.
    I. Response in worship.
III. Iconoclastic introduction.
    A. Divine direction.
    B. Curtain of darkness.
    C. Horrified citizenry.
    D. Fixed blame.
    E. Call for retribution.
    F. Paternal support.
    G. Appropriately renamed.
    H. Midianite mobilization.
IV. The rally call.
    A. Manpower present.
    B. The dew test.
    C. Twofold verification.

CHAPTER 7

I. Battle positions.
    A. Test for sincere humility.
    B. Fearful mustered out.
    C. Further test for divine deliverance.
    D. Commander-in-chief's choice.
II. Command to advance.
    A. Victory assured.
    B. Reconnaissance permitted.
    C. Enemy dream interpretation.
III. Battle strategy.
    A. Abrahamic tactics (cf. Gen 14:14-15).
    B. Three-pronged pincer attack.
    C. Battle blast.
    D. Ruinous rout.
    E. Recruitment of volunteers.
    F. Midianites mitigated in full.

CHAPTER 8

I. National pride.
  A. A reason for exclusion.
  B. Scattered vision.
  C. Anger assuaged by right viewpoint.
II. Lack of reciprocity.
  A. A plea for provisions.
  B. Twofold denial.
  C. Promised punishment.
III. Pursuit payoff.
  A. Quarry found.
  B. Victory odds.
  C. Retributive justice.
  D. Personal responsibility.
IV. Throne spurned.
  A. Right of conquest.
  B. Willing subjects.
  C. Material remembrances.
  D. Satan's attack.
  E. Civic withdrawal.
  F. Licentious living.
  G. Forty years of rest ended.
  H. Short memories.
  I. Past patronage passes.

CHAPTER 9

I. Ambition's drive.
  A. Limited range of authority.
  B. Play on family linkage.
  C. Family endorsement.
  D. Opposition eliminated.
  E. The coronation.
II. The parable of the trees.
  A. The voice of escapee.
  B. Analogy of choice.
  C. Disastrous expectations.
  D. Lesson application.
  E. Recall of past benefits.
  F. Commitment to fate.
III. Sin's pay off.
  A. Treachery's answer to treachery.
  B. Rebel actions.
  C. Retributive measures.
  D. A challenge to leadership.
  E. Resulting conflict.
  F. Short-termed victory.
  G. "Birnum wood"'s march.
  H. Head shrinking.

CHAPTER 10

I. Successive judges.
  A. Issachar background.
  B. Twenty-three year judgeship.
  C. Gileadite judge.
  D. Tenure of twenty-two years.
II. Idolatry returned.
  A. Cousin's invasion.
    1. Moab.
    2. Ammon.
  B. Age-old cry.
  C. Diety's demur.
    1. Review of Israel's reluctance.
    2. Recall of remorse.
    3. Reminder of rebellion.
  D. Sin acknowledged.
  E. Call for leader.

CHAPTER 11

I. Ostracism.
  A. Wandering wantonness.
  B. Family flauntingness.
  C. Wayward wastries.
II. Longing for leadership.
  A. Animosity annulled.
  B. Prestige in perseverance.
  C. Tested truculence.

JUDGES

III. Leadership lambasted.
   A. Arrogant aggression.
   B. Presumptuous claims.
   C. Guilt unclaimed.
IV. Reclamation review.
   A. First advent.
   B. Careful to avoid trespassing.
   C. Circumvented property rights.
   D. Amorite examples.
   E. Belated claim.
   F. Reluctance to assert ownership.
   G. Stubborn resistance.
V. Victory march.
   A. Bolstered by the Spirit.
   B. Vow for victory.
   C. Selfless pledge.
   D. Encouraging encounter.
   E. Complete mastery.
   F. Jarring jubilation.
      1. One of a kind.
      2. Sorrowful submission.
      3. Futile fulfillment.
   G. Lasting lament.

CHAPTER 12

I. Jealous pride.
   A. Pseudo loyalty.
   B. Threats of violence.
   C. Unpleasant reminder.
   D. Relief in self-help only.
II. Jealous conflict.
   A. Pitched battle.
   B. False claims refuted.
   C. Language barrier.
   D. Jephtheh's jurisdiction.
III. Successive jurisprudence.
   A. Seven years of Ibzan.
      1. Family of sixty progeny.
      2. Heterogamous marriages.
   B. Ten years of Elon.
      1. Zebulonite.
      2. Nonmemorable service.
   C. Eight years of Abdon.
      1. Family augmentation.
      2. Unimounted family.

CHAPTER 13

I. Repetitious sin.
   A. Return to the rut.
   B. Forty years of subjection.
II. Remembering Redeemer.
   A. One family of one tribe.
   B. Family limitation overcome.
   C. Familial directives.
   D. Family report.
   E. Family concern.
III. Repeat performance.
   A. Answered prayer.
   B. Confirmed authenticity.
   C. Directions unchanged.
   D. Division of worship discouraged.
   E. Wonders in worship.
   F. Fear from disclosure.
   G. Surcease in logic.
IV. Prescient payoff.
   A. Samson's birth.
   B. Samson's growth.
   C. Samson's empowerment.

CHAPTER 14

I. Man's desire for God's use.
   A. Amorous meandering.
   B. Parental perturbation.
   C. Filial demand response.
II. Implementation inquiry.
   A. Betrothal negotiations.

B. Travel hazards.
   C. Strength sufficient.
   D. Pleasing parley.
III. Completion contract.
   A. Victory site revisited.
   B. Nature's remunerations.
   C. Shared benefits.
   D. Social customs.
   E. Sporting bargaining.
   F. Bargaining pressure.
      1. False accusation.
      2. Forceful threat.
      3. Feminine logic.
      4. Family loyalties.
      5. Riddle riddled.
   G. Spot check.
   H. Paid in another's treasures.
   I. Marital terminus.

CHAPTER 15

I. Futile future.
   A. Shortsighted plans.
   B. Communication lag.
   C. Unacceptable substitute.
II. Family rift outreach.
   A. National punishment.
   B. Inhumane approach.
   C. Wide arsonistic damage.
   D. Concentrated family.
      1. In-law family.
      2. Samson, personally.
      3. Invasion concentration.
   E. Family and tribal impunity.
III. Final episode.
   A. Submission to tribal demand.
   B. Victory from submission.
   C. Crude cruelty.
   D. Thirst in distress.
   E. Dim-viewed faith.
   F. Fountain of waters.

   G. Jurisdiction limits.

CHAPTER 16

I. Strength in spite of weakness.
   A. No condonation for evil.
   B. Subtle conspiracy.
   C. Subterfuge's answer to subtly.
II. Fancy in transition.
   A. Philistine femininity.
   B. Philistine bait.
   C. Philistine bride offer
   D. Philistine frustration.
      1. Amorous by-play.
      2. Recognized falsehoods.
      3. Woman's oldest weapon.
      4. Love's surrender.
   E. Philistine short-term victory.
   F. Philistine premature "party."
   G. Philistine failure.

CHAPTER 17

I. Sticky fingers.
   A. Till tinkering.
   B. Post-curse confession.
   C. Maternal acquiescence.
   D. Derogated dedication.
II. Individual responsibility.
   A. Ambiguous authority.
   B. Added authenticity.
   C. Behooved blessing.

CHAPTER 18

I. Belated benevolence.
   A. Limited land areas.
   B. Reconnaissance record.
      1. Property.
      2. Personnel.

JUDGES

    3. Petition.
    4. Prescience.
II. Isolationists.
    A. Separation.
    B. Self-contained.
    C. Security.
III. Acquisition.
    A. Land dreams.
    B. Covetousness.
    C. Plundered idolatry.
    D. Prestige pull.
IV. Remonstrance.
    A. Innocency in guilt?
    B. Personal plea.
    C. Majority rights.
    D. Minority dejection.
V. Possession.
    A. Isolation disadvantages.
    B. Rebuilding.
    C. Renamed city.
    D. Displaced devotions.

CHAPTER 19

I. Levite's longings.
    A. Wrong woman.
    B. Wanton withdrawal.
    C. Willful withholding.
    D. Went wooingly.
    E. Winsome welcome.
II. Levite's lingerings.
    A. In-law's invitation.
    B. Fulsome feasting.
    C. Stubborn stance.
    D. Seeking shelter.
III. Levite's lacking.
    A. Night's nurturing.
    B. Pressing petition.
    C. Disturbing deportment.
    D. Damsel defamation.

IV. Levite's lamentation.
    A. Decimation in death.
    B. Defiant dismemberment.
    C. Repulsive request.

CHAPTER 20

I. Atrocity's answer.
    A. Army assembled.
    B. Investigated cause.
    C. Full review.
    D. United stand.
    E. Delegated responsibilities.
    F. Force against force.
    G. False security in numbers.
II. Divine counsel sought.
    A. Battle direction.
    B. Strength not in numbers.
    C. Worship in earnest.
    D. Proved strategy tried.
    E. Between two fires.
    F. Israel victorious.
    G. Refugees in retreat.

CHAPTER 21

I. Israel's depletion.
    A. Benjamin survivors few.
    B. Excluded from marriage.
    C. Jabesh-gilead reponsibility.
        1. Absent from punitive war.
        2. Limited extinction.
        3. Limited bride possibilities.
    D. Spoils of war in lieu of gifts.
II. Tribal restoration.
    A. Count restored as twelve.
    B. Census count small.
    C. No central authority.
    D. Personal responsibility.

RUTH

CHAPTER 1
I. Force of famine.
   A. Abraham's pattern.
   B. Acceptable aliens.
   C. Sustenance in sorrow.
   D. Progeny in alien alliances.
II. Bitter sojourn.
   A. Family ties depleted.
   B. Nostalgia in ascendancy.
   C. Parting of the ways.
      1. Release of quasi-ties.
      2. Encouragement for future.
   D. Alien choice.
      1. Family.
      2. People.
      3. God.
   E. Homecoming.

CHAPTER 2
I. Family prosperity.
   A. Wealth in family ties.
   B. Absence of false pride.
   C. Diligence in labor.
   D. Manifold attractiveness.
   E. Good report of worthiness.
II. Family propinquity.
   A. Cognition in benevolence.
   B. Hospitality in action.
   C. Provision for perseverance.
   D. Labor's rewards.
   E. Report of activities.
   F. Mature counsel.

CHAPTER 3
I. Nuptial prenegotiations.
   A. Matronly machinations.
   B. Maidenly demureness.
   C. Acknowledged obligations.
II. Nuptial assurance.
   A. One of two possibilities.
   B. Agreeable acquiescence.
   C. Secrecy needed.
   D. Reputable demeanor.
   E. Generous gift.
      1. Nullifies emptihandedness.
      2. Logic of appearance.

CHAPTER 4
I. Legality established.
   A. Where men pass by.
   B. Proper presentations.
   C. Full implications disclosed.
   D. Publicly proclaimed.
   E. Witnesses present.
   F. Benevolent blessings.
II. Nuptial legality.
   A. Family established.
   B. Heartaches lessened.
   C. Present blessings.
   D. Progenitor importance.
   E. Genealogy in profile.

I SAMUEL

CHAPTER 1

I. Family background.
   A. Tribal descent.
   B. Polygamy practiced.
   C. Progeny denied one wife.
II. Family worship pattern.
   A. Regular annual event.
   B. A family affair.
   C. Favoritism in affections.
   D. Selfish pride propensities.
   E. Grief in denied motherhood.
III. Personal commitment.
   A. Silent sincerity.
   B. Misinterpreted manifestations.
   C. Mild rebuke.
   D. Confessional defense.
   E. Priestly blessing.
   F. Complete worship.
IV. Remembered vow.
   A. Remembered prayer.
   B. Reminder in son's name.
   C. Worship deferred.
   D. Vow fulfillment.
   E. Worship outreach.

CHAPTER 2

I. A prayer in song.
   A. God's anwer to prayer.
   B. God's exclusiveness.
   C. God's exaltation.
      1. Humble man.
      2. Puny Man.
      3. Poverty of man.
   D. God's equity.
   E. God's perseverance.
   F. God's regency.
II. Blood thicker than devoutness.
   A. Sons not like father.
   B. Paternal failure.
      1. Sons ignorant of God.
      2. Selfish in priestly roles.
   C. Despised worship.
      1. Unrestrained greed.
      2. Wantonness in worship.
   D. Mild rebukes.
III. Replacement being groomed.
   A. Samuel's training.
   B. Samuel's home ties.
   C. Samuel's family blessed.
   D. Eli's full warning.
      1. Dismal review.
      2. Predicted poverty of spirit.
      3. Successor selected.
      4. Futile requests.

CHAPTER 3

I. Diligent ministry.
   A. Proper subordination.
   B. Values recognized.
   C. Limitations noted.
   D. Alert to serve.
   E. Repeated calls answered.
   F. Limited knowledge.
II. Diligent mentor.
   A. Mild mannered.
   B. Deliberative perception.
   C. Perceptive counsel.
III. Diligent Deity.
   A. No possible paragon.

- B. Persistent pursuant.
- C. Pungent prophecy.
- D. Fulminating fulfillment.
- IV. Diligent divulgence.
  - A. Reluctance in revelation.
  - B. Pressure for prescience.
  - C. Vicarious vacuity voiced.
  - D. Complete compliance.
  - E. Sanctioned sublimation.
- V. Diligent deportment.
  - A. Accepted acclaim.
  - B. Words of wisdom.
  - C. Selected schedule.

CHAPTER 4

- I. Spokesman for all Israel.
  - A. God's message via Samuel.
  - B. Mobilization call.
  - C. Ebenezer camp.
  - D. Battle positions.
- II. Failure of Israel.
  - A. Battle loss.
  - B. Spirit loss.
  - C. Faith loss.
  - D. Bolster needed.
- III. Courage booster for Israel.
  - A. Presence of the Ark.
  - B. Courage in prospect.
  - C. Courage in backlash.
- IV. False courage for Israel.
  - A. Courage in noise only.
  - B. Power in feet, not hearts.
  - C. Courage symbol lost.
  - D. Prophecy fulfillment.
    1. Eli's sons die.
    2. Eli's death a close second.
  - E. Remembrance continuity.
    1. Birth of fatherless heir.
    2. Heir's name.
  - F. Departed glory.

CHAPTER 5

- I. Misplaced Ark of the Covenant.
  - A. Alien hands.
  - B. Alien temple.
  - C. Alien god's submission.
  - D. Alien temple deserted.
- II. Retaliations of the Ark.
  - A. Physical ailments.
  - B. No city exemption.
  - C. Consternation rampant.
  - D. Futile councils.
  - E. Cries of anguish.

CHAPTER 6

- I. Philistine palaver.
  - A. Ark problem.
  - B. Conference for solution.
  - C. Diviner's device.
    1. Buying favors.
    2. Double reminders.
    3. Foolproof test.
- II. Restoration in action.
  - A. Proper preparations.
  - B. Return route uncharted.
  - C. Rejoicing at point of re-entry.
  - D. Burnt offering in rejoicing.
  - E. Accepted trespass offerings.
  - F. Curious gaze fault.
    1. Unanointed look into ark.
    2. Severe penalty.
    3. Lamentations.
  - G. Plea for release.

CHAPTER 7

- I. Closer home.
  - A. Abinadad home on a hill.

I SAMUEL

  B. Son, Eleazar, a caretaker.
  C. Lack of uniform leadership.
  D. Lament as response.
II. Revival call.
  A. Denounce idols.
  B. True repentance.
  C. Proof of changed lives.
  D. Assembly for dedication.
    1. Sincere worship.
    2. Religious fasting.
    3. Jurisdiction in practice.
III. Threat to safety.
  A. Assembly repercussion.
  B. Aggressive opposition.
  C. Agitated hearts.
  D. A call for prayer support.
  E. Worship approach.
  F. Meteorologic combat.
  G. Routed enemy.
IV. Victory mementoes.
  A. Cleared battlefield.
  B. Ebenezer stone.
  C. Restored cities.
  D. Widespread peace.
  E. Peaceful circuit jurisdiction.

CHAPTER 8

I. Nepotism in jurisprudence.
  A. Qualifications in kinship.
  B. Jurisdiction established.
  C. Perverted justice.
  D. Loss of public patronage.
II. Comparative influence.
  A. Legitimate request.
  B. Shattered hopes.
  C. Neighbor motivation.
  D. Disturbed leadership.
  E. Highest appeal.
III. Rejection placement.

  A. Long standing pattern.
  B. Predicted regal pattern.
    1. Loss of controls.
    2. Loss of personnel.
    3. Loss of property.
    4. Loss of prayer power.
  C. Unyielding demand.
  D. Implementation pattern.

CHAPTER 9

I. Twofold hunt.
  A. Chattel property lost.
  B. Leadership lost (implied).
  C. Different appearance.
  D. Diligent search.
  E. Fruitless effort.
  F. Final prospect.
II. Twofold find.
  A. Twofold report.
    1. Lost chattels located.
    2. Special guest privileges.
    3. Directives in the offing.
  B. Long term implications.
  C. Consternation in humility.
  D. Secretive session.

CHAPTER 10

I. Orientation in private.
  A. Private anointing.
  B. Newscast of past events.
  C. Forecast of immediate future.
  D. Directives for deportment.
  E. Spiritual guidance.
II. Fulfilled predictions.
  A. A new heart.
  B. A new prophet.
  C. A new proverb.
III. Partial allegiance.
  A. Partial itinerary report.

B. Partial events report.
　　C. Partial review of the past.
　　D. Partial obedience to God.
　　E. Partial tribal choice.
　　F. Partial humility.
　　G. Partial acceptance.
　　H. Partial rejection.
　　I. Partial forgiveness.

CHAPTER 11

I. A test of solidarity.
　　A. Aggressor aggravation.
　　B. Limited invasion.
　　C. Rather switch than fight.
　　D. Unreasonable demand.
　　E. Stall for time.
　　F. Call for help.
　　G. Unique call for support.
II. Solidarity in action.
　　A. Full commitment.
　　B. Complete rout.
　　C. Demand for opposition penalty.
　　D. Magnanimity of spirit.
　　E. Kingdom affirmation.
　　F. Unity in offerings.
　　G. United rejoicing.

CHAPTER 12

I. Retirement message.
　　A. Leadership vs. public demand.
　　B. Age's demand.
　　C. Integrity's demand.
　　D. Verified honesty.
　　E. Established record.
II. Recalcitrance in retrospect.
　　A. Exodus beginnings.
　　B. Answered prayers.
　　C. Patulous pattern.
　　D. Chastisement trend.
　　E. Repeated repentances.
　　F. Reminder of responsibility.
　　G. Hopeful future.
III. Retributive revelation.
　　A. Natural phenomenal proof.
　　B. Acknowledged sin.
　　C. Vicarious prayer power.
　　D. Protective projection in obedience.
　　E. Promised prayer support.
　　F. Warning for waywardness.

CHAPTER 13

I. Kingly action???
　　A. Time element.
　　B. Chosen "bodyguard."
　　C. Division of command.
　　D. Vicarious glory.
　　E. Self-advertising.
　　F. Facing danger.
II. Kingly presumption.
　　A. Force of fear.
　　B. Fearful abandonment.
　　C. Impatience in fear.
　　D. Usurpation of priesthood in fear.
　　E. Fear-flavored alibi.
III. King's rejection.
　　A. Foolish reactions.
　　B. Failure in faith.
　　C. Fulmination for disobedience.
　　D. Fulsome desertions.
IV. Kingly limitations.
　　A. Limited territory.
　　B. Limited armaments.
　　C. Limited concessions.
　　D. Limited protection.

CHAPTER 14

I. Brave minority.

I SAMUEL

   A. Adventurous adversary.
   B. Secretive exploit.
   C. Thermopylaic approach.
   D. Useable test plan.
   E. Used opportunities.
II. Reassuring repercussions.
   A. Enemy turmoil.
   B. Lost identity.
   C. Census checkup.
   D. Repatriated quislings.
   E. Rash vow.
III. Rational viewpoint.
   A. Rebuke of vow.
   B. Prodigal refutation.
   C. Sane schedule.
   D. Sacrifice sans sacerdotality.
IV. Irrational battle plans.
   A. Unanswered prayer.
   B. Census for blame.
   C. Rash vow of vituperation.
   D. Jephthahlitic response.
   E. Cancellation by public opinion.
V. Rampaging king.
   A. King in fact and action.
   B. Widespread forays.
   C. A king's familialogy.
   D. A king's genealogy.
   E. Impressment.

CHAPTER 15

I. A second chance.
   A. Call to service recalled.
   B. Right wave length needed.
   C. Special assignment.
      1. Remembered offense.
      2. Delayed punishment.
      3. Specific directions.
II. A right start.
   A. Assembled adequate army.
   B. Aggression prospects.
   C. Magnanimous separation.
   D. Victory over enemy.
III. A wrong compliance.
   A. Partial obedience.
   B. Selfishness in control.
   C. Wrong choice recognized.
   D. A prophet's grief.
   E. A false recount.
   F. A telltale refutation.
   G. Buck-passing.
   H. Distorted sense of values.
   I. Sad announcement.
IV. Retributive justice.
   A. Remorse for sin.
   B. Refused fellowship.
   C. Visual object lesson.
   D. Repentance in worship.
   E. Payment in own measure.
   F. Complete separation.

CHAPTER 16

I. Mourning ends.
   A. New mission.
   B. Directions needed.
   C. A community consternation.
      1. Sacrificial worship.
      2. Family designation.
   D. The eyes of man.
   E. The eyes of God.
   F. Process of elimination.
   G. God's chosen.
II. Spiritual leadership.
   A. Anointing ceremony.
   B. Infilling spirit.
   C. Departing Spirit.
   D. Replacing spirit.
   E. Musical therapy diagnosis.
   F. Introduction to court life.
   G. Personnel demands.
   H. Therapeutic strings.

CHAPTER 17

I. Battle arrangements.
   A. Strategic heights.
   B. Field for action.
   C. Challenger-show-off.
   D. Power of size.
   E. Terror victory.
II. Battle adjournment.
   A. Lack of daring.
   B. Home interest.
   C. Messenger of concern.
   D. Fraternal jealousy.
   E. Minority diffidence.
   F. Healthy curiosity.
   G. Honest pledge.
   H. Confidence report.
   I. Levels of preparation.
III. Battle action.
   A. Disdainful reception.
      1. Immaturity.
      2. Lack of experience.
      3. Plebeian weapons.
   B. Exchange of challenges.
   C. The courage of faith.
   D. Arms extension.
   E. Singular victory.
   F. Fire touches fire.
   G. Surprising consequences.
   H. Memory's limitation.
   I. Humility's crown.

CHAPTER 18

I. Budding friendship.
   A. Courage answered courage.
   B. Equitable esteem.
   C. Acclaimed by accouterments.
   D. Recognized reliability.
   E. Performance pattern.
II. Blighted friendship.
   A. Song themes.
   B. Juggernaut of jealousy.
   C. Evil intent.
   D. Fuel to hatred.
   E. Loss of public image.
III. Blasted friendship.
   A. Set snares.
   B. Redirected subterfuge.
   C. Subtle use of sentiment.
   D. Foiled machinations.
   E. Embroiling enmity.

CHAPTER 19

I. Reprieve by request.
   A. Rash requisition.
   B. Close-lipped conference.
   C. Logical liaison.
      1. Realistic review.
      2. Revenge requited.
   D. Reported reprieve.
   E. Restored relationship.
II. Reprieve revoked.
   A. War renewal.
   B. Victorious leadership.
   C. Recurrent evil spirit.
   D. Therapeutic magnanimity.
   E. Projected pusillanimity.
III. Preprieve relayed.
   A. Love's leniency.
   B. Love's labor.
   C. Love's lackey.
   D. Love's lair.
   E. Love's lamination.

CHAPTER 20

I. Reconnaissance.
   A. Reasoned reckoning.
   B. Reasonable response.
   C. Reticence recognized.
   D. Review of remiss.
II. Projected procedure.
   A. Observing eyes.
   B. Listening ears.
   C. Traumatic tongue.

I SAMUEL

    D. Punctuated argument.
       1. Eve-atic blame.
       2. Logical question.
       3. Illogical answer.
       4. Unreasonable reaction.
III. Patterned compliance.
    A. A clear message.
    B. Friendship re-vowed.
    C. Separated friends.

CHAPTER 21

I. Fugitive fleeing.
    A. Priestly protection.
    B. Priestly precaution.
    C. Priestly provisions.
       1. Food.
       2. Armament.
II. Fugitive fudging.
    A. Enemy territory.
    B. Enemy recognition.
    C. Enemy disdain.

CHAPTER 22

I. Escapee's convergence.
    A. Rallying leader.
    B. Rallying reasons.
    C. Refuge request.
    D. Moab mandate.
    E. Gadabout advice of Gad.
II. Geyseritic jealousy.
    A. False fulminations.
    B. Pyschosomatic prying.
    C. Selfish shortsighted subservience.
    D. Harsh harassment.
    E. Vicarious virtue.
III. Demented deportment.
    A. Defaming decimation declared.
    B. Defense in demurral.
    C. Doeg, the do-good decimator.
    D. Dedicated decried.
    E. Unity in unacceptance.

CHAPTER 23

I. SOS from Keilah.
    A. Harvest raiders.
    B. Fear answering distress.
    C. Prayer for guidance.
    D. Relief in victory.
II. Payoff from Keilah.
    A. Symbol of inquiry.
    B. Threat of apprehension.
    C. Besiege danger.
    D. Loss of gratitude.
III. Removal from Keilah.
    A. Wilderness safety.
    B. Friendship's dividends.
       1. Conference.
       2. Confidence.
       3. Covenant.
    C. CIA reports.
    D. Selfish commendation.
    E. Spy palaver.
    F. Mountain safety.
    G. Helpful invasion.
    H. Engedi stronghold.

CHAPTER 24

I. Duo-return.
    A. Philistine hunt ended.
    B. Hunt for David resumed.
    C. Proximity of danger.
    D. Opportunity for revenge.
II. Duo-interpretation.
    A. Evidence of magnanimity.
    B. Support of logic.
    C. Presentation of proof.
    D. Pseudo syllogistic argument.

- E. Pseudo uncertainty in recognition.
- F. Pseudo confession.
- G. Cognizance of certainty.
- H. Sincere concession.
- I. Continued wariness.

CHAPTER 25

I. Samuel succumbs.
   - A. National mourning.
   - B. Family funeral place.
   - C. David's itinerary.
II. Meal time.
   - A. Background source.
   - B. Adequate supply.
   - C. Reciprocal reverberations.
   - D. Respectful request.
   - E. Rude rebuff.
III. Reverse measures.
   - A. No protection sans provisions.
   - B. Preventative proclamation.
   - C. Forestalling food offering.
   - D. Deductive dedication.
   - E. Frank favoritism.
IV. Rewarding results.
   - A. Adequate acquiesence.
   - B. Adroit admission.
   - C. Heart failure.
   - D. Enemy extricated.
   - E. Thanksgiving for Divine protection.
   - F. Who rewards whom?

CHAPTER 26

I. Ziph squealers.
   - A. Hiding place revealed.
   - B. Over-powered foray.
   - C. Counter spying.
II. Strategy in ironity.
   - A. Valiantly guarded.
      1. Appurtenances.
      2. Supernatural deep sleep.
   - B. Inhibited by integrity.
   - C. Evidence of restraint.
   - D. Ironic upbraiding.
   - E. Paternal recognition.
   - F. On the spot logic.
      1. Exaggerated transient gains.
      2. Questionable motivation.
      e. Futile flea hunt.
III. Remorse in confession.
   - A. Recognized sin.
   - B. Invitation for reconciliation.
   - C. Plea for reciprocity.
   - D. Continued separation.

CHAPTER 27

I. Self-exiled.
   - A. Hopeless sanctuary in Israel.
   - B. In the enemy's camp.
   - C. Political asylum.
   - D. Saul dissuaded by "newscast."
II. Cruel strategy.
   - A. Israel's enemies as victims.
   - B. Sustenance by spoils.
   - C. No talebearers.
   - D. False reports.
   - E. Blind acceptance.

CHAPTER 28

I. War clouds.
   - A. Philistines on the rampage.
   - B. David's band "inducted."
   - C. A poignant loss remembered.

II SAMUEL

    D. Craven conscience.
II. War council.
    A. Forbidden counseloress.
    B. Nocturnal conclave.
    C. Subterfuge in request.
    D. Disturbing results.
        1. Identity revelations.
        2. Fruitless efforts.
        3. Profound prognostications.
        4. Spiritless survival.
    E. Feminine fancies.

CHAPTER 29

I. Achish accosted.
    A. A quisling in camp?
    B. Divided sentiment.
II. David deferred.
    A. Achish's apology.
    B. Achish's approval.
    C. Achish's advice.
    D. Achish apart from David.

CHAPTER 30

I. Saddened survivors.
    A. Gathering grief.
    B. Grief-flavored blame.
    C. Prayer for guidance.
    D. Assuring answer.

   II. Revenge reconnaissance.
      A. Limits to strength.
      B. Divided forces.
      C. Helpful contact.
      D. Valuable guide.
   III. Retribution in action.
      A. Surcease in complete victory.
      B. Complete recovery of families.
      C. Added spoils.
      D. Triumphant return.
   IV. Equitable spoils system.
      A. Selfishness overruled.
      B. Division of responsibility rewards.
      C. Precedent set.
      D. Presents to Israel's elders.

CHAPTER 31

   I. Saul's last battle.
      A. Israel's retreating rout.
      B. Saul sought.
      C. Saul's wound.
      D. Saul's command.
      E. Saul's suicide.
      F. Saul's sons.
   II. Israel's plight.
      A. Full retreat.
      B. King's defamation.
      C. Idol's honor.
      D. Jabesh-gilead's reverence.

II SAMUEL

CHAPTER 1

I. Battle report.
    A. David's informer.
    B. Oriental grief sighs.
    C. Full summary.
    D. Hope for commendation.
    E. Grief period lengthened.
II. Mourning augmented.
    A. Bragger bunco-ed.
    B. Logical decision.
    C. Regal requiem.
    D. Love's lament.

CHAPTER 2
I. Kingdom projections.
   A. Kingless regime.
   B. Divine guidance.
   C. Residence established.
   D. Tribal acceptance.
   E. Regal acclaim to Jabesh-gilead.
   F. Regnant patronage.
II. Kingdom rivalry.
   A. Army coup d'etat.
   B. Divided kingdom.
   C. Confrontation.
   D. Saulites in retreat.
   E. Ambitious youth.
      1. Speed.
      2. Persistence.
      3. Warning disregarded.
      4. Self-protection.
III. Kingdom war recess.
   A. Call to consider.
   B. Bilateral covenant.
   C. Homecomings.

CHAPTER 3
I. War records.
   A. Time growth.
   B. Kingdom growth.
   C. Family growth.
II. War developments.
   A. Generalship.
   B. General defamed.
   C. General in rebuff.
   D. General in threat.
III. War transference.
   A. Conference requested.
   B. Conference price.
   C. Conference concluded.
   D. United Israel possible.
IV. War vengeance.
   A. Military resurgence.
   B. Questions authority.
   C. Action sans real sanction.
   D. Vengeance backlash.
      1. Personal vengeance.
      2. Regal displeasure.
      3. Populace conformity.
      4. Divine judgment, the last word.

CHAPTER 4
I. Political propensity.
   A. Courage depletion.
   B. Conniving conspirators.
   C. Family implications.
   D. Inept inactivity.
   E. Political profit?
II. Political backfire.
   A. Plight of former favor seeker.
   B. Repetitious retribution.
   C. Cruel punishment.
   D. Rescinding effort.

CHAPER 5
I. Unifying overtures.
   A. Tribal unanimity.
   B. Ethnic logic.
   C. National kingship.
   D. Chronologic chart.
II. Capital plans.
   A. Jerusalem possibilities.
   B. Inhabitants restrictions.
   C. Five-star general goal.
   D. The city of David.
   E. Propitious progress.
III. International recognition.
   A. Zidonian zeal for friendship.
   B. Polygamy and population explosion.
   C. Polyglot Philistine propinquities.
   D. Deity directed.

II SAMUEL

1. Instantaneous action.
2. Delay for precise instant.
3. Complete rout.

CHAPTER 6

I. Worship symbol.
   A. The Ark out of place.
   B. Preparation for removal.
   C. Lack of research.
   D. Copy of heathen ignorance.
II. Worship thwarted.
   A. Undedicated hands.
   B. Severe reminder of nonconsecrated.
   C. Postponed continuation.
   D. Temporary sanctuary.
   E. Precious presence.
III. Worship unrestrained.
   A. Original motivation.
   B. Original method.
   C. Overmuch zeal.
   D. Adoration in abandonment.
IV. Worship unappreciated.
   A. Selfish decorum.
   B. Social prestige concern.
   C. Egoistic logic.
   D. Preferment emphasized.
   E. Limited blessings.

CHAPTER 7

I. Reverent relevancy.
   A. Cedar-housed king.
   B. Curtain-housed God.
   C. Perception approved by man.
   D. Presumption of man.
   E. Prescribed procedure of God.
II. Projected plans.
   A. Divine architect.
   B. Past performances.
   C. Planned purpose.
   D. Purposeful "planting."
   E. National entity.
III. Promised protection.
   A. Dynasty determined.
      1. Contingent on obedience.
      2. Chastisement as needed.
      3. Lasting mercy.
   B. Established (fixed) kingdom.
   C. Reliable messenger.
IV. Prayer pliancy.
   A. Humility in compliance.
   B. Present status appreciation.
   C. Prognostication unparalleled.
   D. National singularity.
   E. Unrefutable proof.
   F. Complete commitment.
   G. Uncompromising surrender.

CHAPTER 8

I. Majestic measures.
   A. Philistia measured short.
   B. Moab measured by line.
   C. Outreach measured to Euphrates.
   D. Enemy's ally measured.
II. Majestic magnanimity.
   A. Sanctified spoils.
   B. Glorified gifts.
   C. Regal reign.
   D. Delegated departments.

CHAPTER 9
I. Royal remembrance.
   A. Friendship's inquiry.
   B. Friendship's humility.
   C. Friendship's logic.
II. Friendship in fulfillment.
   A. Patrimony provisions.
   B. Assigned allegiance.
   C. Assignment accepted.
   D. Permanent guest.

CHAPTER 10
I. Diplomacy denounced.
   A. Condolence commitment.
   B. Malevolent interpretation.
   C. Humiliating reception.
   D. Face-saving directive.
   E. Guilty conscience conspiracy.
II. Diplomatic designs.
   A. Force meets force.
   B. Panzer provision.
   C. Undiplomatic unctions.
   D. Repercussive chain-reaction.
   E. Deliverance.
III. Diplomatic capitulation.

CHAPTER 11
I. Unkingly kinks.
   A. Lolling leisure.
   B. Vicarious valiance.
   C. Insidious insomnia.
   D. Seducing sight.
   E. Wounding wantonness.
   F. Jarring gravemen.
II. Bungling Bunco.
   A. Specified reporter.
   B. Pseudo-inquiry.
   C. Furlough privileges.
   D. Kingly k-rations.
III. Thwarted truncheon.
   A. The soldier inhibitions.
   B. The soldier enigma.
   C. The soldier heart.
   D. Extended soldier's pass.
   E. Devious devices.
IV. Autocratic authority.
   A. Death warrant carrying victim.
   B. Chain of command.
   C. Complete compliance.
   D. Precaution in report.
   E. Stoical appraisal.
   F. Discrete mourning.
   G. Complete conquest of heart?

CHAPTER 12
I. Personal parable.
   A. Contrast in possessions.
   B. Contrast in animal husbandry.
   C. Crass cupidity.
   D. Purely objective judgment.
II. The pungent placement.
   A. Pointed peroration.
   B. Guilt gilded.
   C. Remonstrative reticence.
   D. Sin syndrome.
   E. Promised peril perpetuity.
III. Accepted acrimony.
   A. Acknowledged abominations.
   B. Forgiveness forthcoming.
   C. Primal punishment.
IV. Vestibule to vengeance.
   A. Terminal illness.
   B. Traumatic tension.
   C. Persistent prayer.
   D. Prescient perception.
   E. Unprecedented reaction.
   F. Philosophical logic.
V. Reaction for restoration.

II SAMUEL

A. Mourning assuaged.
B. Active motherhood.
C. Divine approval.
D. Warfare outlet.
E. Chain of command.
F. Victors' spoils.

CHAPTER 13

I. Inordinate desire.
  A. Unconcealed demeanor.
  B. Unwise device.
  C. Insidious demand.
  D. Incestuous duress.
  E. Unmerited despisement.
II. Uncontrolled disdain.
  A. Isolated desolation.
  B. Invitational derogation.
  C. Insidious deportment.
  D. Inglorious demise.
  E. Innocuous declarations.
III. Inimical departure.
  A. International defenses.
  B. Intemperate delineation.
  C. Ingrained deluge.
  D. Inured depression.

CHAPTER 14

I. Subordinate's subtrafuge.
  A. Masqueraded accomplice.
  B. Faked petition.
  C. Strained analogy.
  D. Gullible king.
  E. Direct application.

II. Public pressure.
  A. Felt affront.
  B. Spokesman's presentation.
  C. God's example.
  D. King's wisdom.
  E. King's mentor.
  F. King's integrity.
III. Astute insight.
  A. King's discernment.
  B. King's question.
  C. King's enlightenment.
  D. King's acquiescence.
  E. King's command.
IV. Restricted repatriation.
  A. Obeisance in gratitude.
  B. Pleasing assignment.
  C. Return sans audience.
  D. Compliance in part.
  E. Public reputation.
  F. Family man.
  G. Posterity petulance.
  H. Naive action.
  I. Arm-twisting demands.
  J. Filial restoration.

CHAPTER 15

I. Ambitious ingratitude.
  A. Show of authority.
  B. Ingratiating politicking.
  C. Campaign promises.
  D. Handshaking, "baby"-kissing politician.
  E. Successful campaign.
II. Paradox of plea and purpose.
  A. Spurious reason.
  B. Selfish interpretation.
  C. Subservient surreptitiousness.
  D. Innocent vanguard.
  E. A quisling enlisted.
  F. Rebel increase.
III. Disturbing declaration.
  A. Heart harvest opposition.
  B. Retreat strategy.
  C. Live-property saving withdrawal.
  D. Loyal following.
  E. Alien loyalty despite exemption.
  F. Safe separation.
IV. Designed deflections.
  A. Priesthood and the Ark.

    B. Re-establishment.
    C. Reliance on Divine direction.
    D. Listening ears.
    E. Quislingism reported.
    F. Prayer for misinterpretation.
    G. Espionage established.

CHAPTER 16

  I. Help from "enemy" camp.
    A. Servant of first dynasty crown prince.
    B. Timely transportation.
    C. Pertinent provisions.
    D. Loyalty to royalty.
  II. Cursings and castings.
    A. Kicking a downed dog.
    B. Persistent pertinacity.
    C. Accepted accusations.
    D. Expected expiation.
    E. Refreshing pause.
  III. Plausible patronage.
    A. Questioned allegiance.
    B. Regal goal for fealty.
    C. Priority preference.
    D. Personal perfidy.
    E. Answered prayer.

CHAPTER 17

  I. Psychological warfare.
    A. Status seekers.
    B. Plan of strategy.
    C. First acceptance.
    D. Comfort counsel.
    E. Comfirmation sought.
    F. Vacillating rebel.
    G. Face-saving suicide.
  II. WAC involvement.
    A. Out of uniform.
    B. Courier service.
    C. Undercover subterfuge.
    D. Half-truths.
    E. Mission accomplished.
  III. Battle strategy.
    A. Withdrawal for consolidation.
    B. Rebel generalship.
    C. Subservient supplier.
    D. Consolation commissary.

CHAPTER 18

  I. Organized for defense.
    A. Necessary head count.
    B. Delegated authority.
    C. Scattered "eggs."
    D. Regal ambition.
    E. Popular demand.
    F. Kingly consent.
    G. Paternal concern.
  II. Pitched battle.
    A. Natural armament.
    B. Israel's rebel losses.
    C. Timbercraft enemy.
    D. Rebel leader "timberized."
    E. Paternal safeguards.
    F. "Five-star" general's disregard.
    G. Rebel leader's remembrance (v. 18).
  III. Rebellion ended (v. 16).
    A. Dismissal trumpet.
    B. Messenger competition.
    C. Wishful forecast.
    D. Partial report.
    E. Full implications.
    F. A father's grief.

CHAPTER 19

  I. Personal grief.
    A. A father's heart.
    B. A general's concern.
    C. A jarring introspection.
    D. A true evaluation of actions.

II SAMUEL

   E. A conference for allegiance.
II. Personal retrospection.
   A. Remembrances by the *populous*.
   B. Church and state ties.
   C. Planned demotion.
   D. A quisling's apology.
   E. A benevolent pardon.
   F. A half-true alibi.
   G. A benefactor's invitation.
   H. A vicarious receiver.
III. Personal disunity.
   A. Blood thicker than water.
   B. Ratio of allegiance.
   C. Triumph of tribal ties.

CHAPTER 20

I. Rebel echoes.
   A. Evil usurpation.
   B. Former dynasty loyalty.
   C. Mob reaction.
II. Rebel remunerations.
   A. Regality on the return.
   B. Rebuke in isolation.
   C. Installation preparation.
   D. Mission against rebels.
   E. Jealous subtlety.
   F. Fatal naivete.
   G. Backfired presumption.
III. Rebel termination.
   A. Besieged refuge.
   B. Bilateral parley.
   C. Siege-lift price paid.
   D. Political reorganization.

CHAPTER 21

I. Natural retaliation.
   A. One man's sin widespread.
   B. Tribal choice allowed.
   C. Beyond monetary value.
   D. Complete recompense demanded.
   E. Maternal love and respect.
   F. Past due rites.
II. Renewed conflicts.
   A. Age-old aggression.
   B. Champion of giants.
   C. Loyalty restrictions.
   D. The last of the giants.

CHAPTER 22 (restated in Psalm 18)

(outline of Psalm 18 from THE PSALMS IN OUTLINE, copywrited by Baker Book House Company, 1965. Used by permission.)

I. My Lord.
   A. Object of love.
   B. Source of strength.
   C. Sure foundation.
   D. Supplier of every good (need).
   E. Protector.
      1. Refuge.
      2. Shield.
      3. Stronghold.
   F. Deliverer.
      1. Praiseworthy.
      2. Promised relief.
   G. Savior.
   H. Needs expressed to Him.
      1. Bound by death.
      2. Floods of evil.
      3. Bonds of hell ensnared.
      4. Death threatens.
   I. Voiced cry to Him.
      1. For help.
      2. Heard.
      3. Assured answered.
II. My earth in my Lord's hand.
   A. Shook and trembled.

            1. Disciplined.
            2. Punitory.
    B. Volcanic disturbance.
        1. Fire and smoke.
        2. Purification.
        3. Glow still felt.
    C. God is above the heavens.
        1. Power to control.
        2. Descended.
    D. God is above darkness.
        1. Can dispel.
        2. Can use.
    E. Omnipresent God.
        1. Moves swiftly.
        2. Abides everywhere.
        3. Always a pavilion.
    F. Storms of purpose.
        1. Lightnings and thunder.
        2. Hail and rain.
    G. Earth's secrets revealed.
III. My redemption.
    A. God's exaltation.
        1. Far above.
        2. Antithesis to my depths.
    B. God's graciousness.
        1. Came where I was.
        2. Lifted me from the flood.
        3. Delivered me from enemy.
            a. Strong enemy.
            b. Victim of hate.
            c. Unable to save self.
            d. Attacked when down.
        4. Underneath are the everlasting ARMS.
        5. Safe conduct to "broad places."
            a. Room to expand.
            b. Farther from enemy.
        6. He delighted in me.
    C. God's wage scale.
        1. Value received.
        2. Clean hands.
        3. Strait — straight walk.
        4. Devout worship.
        5. Right guide.
        6. Free from condemnation.
IV. Divine characteristics.
    A. Divine reciprocity.
        1. Loyalty paid with loyalty.
        2. Blameless have example in Deity.
        3. Pure and outclass all.
        4. Crooked met opposition.
    B. Divine equalization.
        1. Humbled delivered.
        2. Haughty abased.
        3. Becomes light in darkness.
        4. Overcomes opposition.
        5. Overcomes obstacles.
    C. Divine supremacy.
        1. Way is perfect.
        2. Promise is true.
        3. Protection is complete.
        4. Authority is acknowledged.
V. The Lord is the only God.
    A. A sure Rock.
    B. Gives strength.
    C. Established my way.
        1. Made way perfect.
        2. Made me sure-footed.
        3. Made me able to climb.

I KINGS

      4. Made territory larger.
- D. Teaches self-defenses.
  1. My hands to war.
  2. Strength to break bow of steel.
  3. Upheld by His Right Hand.
  4. Courage to pursue enemy.
  5. Complete victory.
- E. Delivered from strife.
- F. Made ruler over many.
  1. A new dominion.
  2. Cognizance means subjection.
- G. The Lord lives.
  1. Be exalted.
  2. Give thanks.
  3. Praise Him.
- H. The Lord rules.
  1. Through His anointed.
  2. Throughout eternity.

CHAPTER 23

I. Postlude to glory.
  - A. Identity of spokesman.
  - B. Identity of Power Source.
  - C. Identity of Sovereignty.
  - D. Analogy of beginnings.
  - E. Humble limitations.
  - F. Warning against antagonists.

II. Roster of heroes.
  - A. War valor.
  - B. Duty beyond weariness.
  - C. Chauvinistic loyalty.
  - D. Evaluation of risks.
  - E. Differentiation by exploits.
  - F. Census count.

CHAPTER 24

I. Punishment via arrogancy.
  - A. Urge to boastfulness.
  - B. Power sought in numbers.
  - C. Cynical census bureau.
  - D. Time and tally.

II. Punishment by remorse.
  - A. Personal guilt.
  - B. Prayer for forgiveness.
  - C. Acknowledged iniquity.
  - D. A morning of decision.

III. Punishment by choice.
  - A. Natural causes.
  - B. Active antagonists.
  - C. Divine prerogative.
  - D. Remorse for vicarious guilt.
  - E. Deflated ego.

IV. Punishment purged.
  - A. Heart guided worship.
  - B. The worship site at the line of advance.
  - C. Worship sans vicariousness.
  - D. Personal commitment.

I KINGS

CHAPTER 1

I. Regal debility.
  - A. Geriatric Therapeutics.
  - B. Special practical nurse.
  - C. Strictly patonic service.

II. Premature precoronation rites.
  - A. Practical procedures.
  - B. Brother by blood only.
  - C. Army sanction.
  - D. Religious leader support.
  - E. Adroit exemptions.

III. Strategic counter committee.
   A. Prophet chairmanship.
   B. Maternal support.
   C. Previous promise bolster.
   D. Full report on opposition.
   E. Final authority clincher.
   F. Avouchment by chairman.
   G. Guest list exclusions.
   H. Petition pay-off.
IV. Royal reclamation.
   A. Divine record review.
   B. Divine sanction evoked.
   C. Regal coronation authority.
   D. Committee approval.
   E. "FBI" blessing.
   F. Coronation complete.
V. Regality reaffirmed.
   A. Paternal blessing.
   B. Popularity with populus.
   C. Cause for fear.
   D. Sanctuary refuge.
   E. Benign pardon.

CHAPTER 2

I. A royal charge to regality.
   A. Resignation to inevitable.
   B. First loyalty to God.
   C. Prosperity contingent.
      1. Full obedience.
      2. Binding covenant.
   D. Specific affairs of state.
      1. Joab's arrogancy.
      2. Gileadite rewards.
      3. A quisling's retribution.
   E. David's demise.
   F. Chronical summary.
III. A kingly demeanor.
   A. Established domain.
   B. Matriarchal import fashioned.
   C. Egotistical logic faced.
   D. Debasing demand affront.
   E. Improper precedent implied.
IV. Regal authority.
   A. Incestuous inclination inhibited.
   B. Priesthood deposed.
   C. A quisling quelled.
   D. Selfishness vs. safety.
   E. Supreme demesne.

CHAPTER 3

I. Diplomatic alliance.
   A. Royal marriage.
   B. Honeymoon "cottage."
   C. Projected building plans.
   D. Varied worship sites.
   E. Sincere regal worship.
II. Dream revelation.
   A. Test in request.
   B. Honest review.
   C. Humble dependence.
   D. Frank limitation acceptance.
   E. Wise request.
III. Divine approval.
   A. Pleased response.
   B. Fulfilled grant.
      Threefold augmentation.
      1. Riches.
      2. Honor.
      3. Contingent long life.
   D. Worshipful experience.
IV. Wisdom in action.
   A. Confession for background.
   B. Conflicting claims.
   C. Confusion without proof.
   D. Equitable judgment.
   E. Real maternity triumphant.
   F. Popularity in profusion.

I KINGS

CHAPTER 4
I. Regal deployed authority.
   A. Designated tribal leadership.
   B. Innumerable population.
   C. Extended borders.
II. Royal menange provisions.
   A. Abundant amounts.
   B. Adequate tribute.
   C. Kingly arrogancy violates restrictions.
      1. Multiplied horse power.
      2. Temptation to bypass Deity.
   D. No lack for man or beast.
III. Regal endowments.
   A. Incomparable acumen.
   B. No peer in learning.
   C. Prolific writer.
   D. Broad subject matter.
   E. Worldwide acclaim.

CHAPTER 5
I. Bilateral exchanges.
   A. Mutual admiration.
   B. Reciprocal helpfulness.
   C. God's providence.
   D. Building plans.
II. Mutual Pact.
   A. Appropriate skills.
   B. Wages in kind.
   C. Designated responsibilities.
   D. Contract terms approved.
   E. Wisdom's outreach.
III. Work schedules.
   A. Conscripted labor force.
   B. Rotation service periods.
   C. Distributed work load.
   D. Detailed overseers.
   E. Varied craftsmen.

CHAPTER 6
I. Building program.
   A. Chronological placement.
   B. Temple construction.
   C. Architectural conformity.
   D. Practical floor plan.
   E. Prefabricated construction.
   F. Cedar paneling.
   G. Full use of materials.
II. Building aesthetics.
   A. Acceptable with God.
   B. Intricate wood carvings.
   C. Gold overlay.
   D. Imposing enlargement in oracle.
   E. Stone carvings.
   F. Seven year project.

CHAPTER 7
I. Personal building project.
   A. Magnitude in time.
   B. Magnitude in dimensions.
   C. Magnitude in operational floor plan.
II. Metalurgical skill imported.
   A. Tribal ancestry.
   B. Paternal apprenticeship.
   C. Moldings and carvings.
   D. Artificer in grandeur.
III. Appurtenances for worship.
   A. Decorative supports.
   B. Cleansing fount.
   C. Imposing mountings.
   D. Symbolic engravings.
   E. Abundant lavers.
   F. Altar aids.
   G. Totals unaccounted for.
   H. Complete dedication.

CHAPTER 8
I. Temple initiated into service.

- A. National assemblage.
- B. The oracle complete.
- C. Innumerable sacrifices.
- D. Deity's cloud.
- E. Deity's glory.
II. Temple dedication.
- A. God's prerogative.
- B. Choice of dwelling.
- C. Man's deference.
- D. God's supervisions.
- E. God's selection of builder.
- F. Covenant implications.
III. Dedication prayer.
- A. Plea for inviolate covenant.
- B. God's magnitude.
- C. God's condescension.
- D. Man's frailties.
- E. Kingly intercession.
- F. Repentant realities.
- G. Kingly blessing.
IV. Dedicatory sacrifices.
- A. Peace offerings.
- B. Vast number of offerings.
- C. Solemn national feast.
- D. Glad response.

CHAPTER 9

I. Dedication answer.
- A. Divine acceptance.
- B. Divine requirements.
- C. Divine promises.
- D. Divine warning.
II. Dedication annulment possible.
- A. Vagrant king.
- B. Straying people.
- C. Departed glory.
- D. Vivid testimony of ruin.
III. Displeasing payoff.
- A. No commensurate with service.
- B. Continuum in regional name.

- C. Tax schedule
IV. Daughter's dowry.
- A. Gift of father king.
- B. Husband's building project.
V. Deployed work force.
- A. Canaanite bondmen.
- B. Exemption of Israel.
- C. Israelite foremen.
- D. *Camelot* building program.
- E. Developed merchant marine.
- F. Emigrant sailors.

CHAPTER 10

I. International reputation.
- A. Foreign queen *inquisition*.
- B. "Pomp and circumstance."
- C. Unpretentious display.
- D. Highest quiz test score.
- E. Skepticism answered.
- F. Sovereign blessing.
- G. Gifts in gratitude.
II. International exchange.
- A. Navy commerce.
- B. Mementoes of increase.
- C. Guest gifts not small.
- D. Open market trade.
- E. Gamut of merchandise.
III. International patronage.
- A. Wisdom as a commodity.
- B. Assumed responsibilities.
- C. Tangible assets.
- D. The precious made common.
- E. Price stability.

CHAPTER 11

I. Marital instability.
- A. Wisdom fails.
- B. Insecurity intrigues.
- C. Love or lust?

I KINGS

  D. Senility on ascendancy.
  E. Idolatry, a natural step.
  F. Errant sonship.
  G. Follower — not a leader.
II. Displeased Deity.
  A. A day of reckoning prescribed.
  B. Covenant remembrances.
  C. Diminished glory.
  D. Adversaries aroused.
  E. Dubious Egyptian reliability.
  F. Damascene sanctuary.
  G. Foreman defection.
III. Deity's design.
  A. Analogous spokesman.
  B. Subjective implications.
  C. Power of choice limited.
  D. Power of choice portentous.
  E. Promised providence.
  F. Saul-pattern in Solomon.
IV. Dynasty diminishes.
  A. A matter of record.
  B. Chronology fixed.
  C. The passing pattern.

CHAPTER 12

I. Official orientation.
  A. National assembly grounds.
  B. Call for champion.
  C. Petition for relief.
  D. Contingent loyalty.
II. Patriciate in practice.
  A. Veneration for elders.
  B. Sound advice.
  C. Youthful power grab.
  D. Youth in regality.
III. Self-separation.
  A. Retaliatory tax measure.
  B. Retaliatory tax refusal.
  C. Regality in retreat.
  D. Rebel leadership.
  E. Ahijah's prophecy fulfilled.
IV. Sanctioned separation.
  A. Plans for forced reunion.
  B. Induction complete.
  C. Divine purpose revealed.
  D. Army mustered out.
V. Regal pride.
  A. First in politics.
  B. Religion and the state.
  C. Power of exile experiences.
  D. Pattern for Israel.
  E. King appointed priesthood.
  F. Copy of Judah rites.

CHAPTER 13

I. A call for repentance.
  A. Direct mission to apostate king.
  B. Defamation prediction.
  C. A king's disbelief.
  D. A reminder of power source.
  E. A petition for restoration.
  F. A futile invitation.
  G. A circumscribed mission.
II. Starved fellowship.
  A. Stirred by newscast.
  B. Outreach of kindred soul.
  C. Invitation for fellowship.
  D. Restrictions reiterated.
  E. Removal in falsehood.
  F. No safety in false belief.
  G. A Judas confession.
III. Proof of truth.
  A. Resumed journey interrupted.
  B. Unnatural natural phenomenon.

- C. Late newscast.
- D. A borrowed grave.
- E. Sepulcher to share.
- F. Worthy remembrance.
- G. Accepted prophecy.
- IV. Refractory regality.
  - A. Continued apostasy.
  - B. Inappropriate priesthood.
  - C. Sin in continuum.
  - D. Embryo of finality.

CHAPTER 14

- I. A king's limitations.
  - A. Reminder in similarity in son's name.
  - B. Petticoat courier.
  - C. Subterfuge for success.
  - D. Spiritual sight sufficient.
- II. The reason for rejection.
  - A. Disregard for divine directives.
  - B. Reciprocal retribution.
  - C. Dynasty terminus.
  - D. Derogatory simile.
  - E. Animal bait prospect.
  - F. Mission miasma.
  - G. Prognosticated captivity.
  - H. Fulfilled prediction.
  - J. A king's demise.
- III. Parallel happenings.
  - A. Canaanitish maternal background.
  - B. Devious devotions.
  - C. Idolatry over-shadow.
  - D. National defense depleted.
  - E. National treasure loot.
  - F. Inferior replacements.
  - G. Lifelong fraternal enmity.
  - H. A change of kings.

CHAPTER 15

- I. Like son — like father (cf. II Chron. 10-12).
  - A. Power of example.
  - B. Spared by Davidic covenant.
  - C. Continued enmity.
- II. Reverted pattern.
  - A. Recreant to ancestoral idolatry.
  - B. Queen demotion for grandmother.
  - C. Limited reforms.
  - D. Sincere dedication.
- III. Ancestoral groove.
  - A. Antagonistic to Israel.
  - B. Boughten protection.
  - C. Appropriated building material.
  - D. Physical debility.
- IV. Contemporary vagaries.
  - A. Israel's old rut.
  - B. Intrigue and usurpation.
  - C. Complete dynasty change.
  - D. Still in the sin road.

CHAPTER 16

- I. Another chance.
  - A. Prophetic warning.
  - B. Review of providence.
  - C. Like punishment for like evil.
  - D. Crown prince reigns.
- II. Army coup d'etat.
  - A. Chariot captain conspirator.
  - B. Booze as an ally.
  - C. Retaliation possibility prevented.
  - D. Duo-monarchy.
  - E. Rebel removal.
- III. Reunited Israel.
  - A. Building program.
  - B. New capital city.

I KINGS

CHAPTER 4

I. Regal deployed authority.
   A. Designated tribal leadership.
   B. Innumerable population.
   C. Extended borders.

II. Royal menange provisions.
   A. Abundant amounts.
   B. Adequate tribute.
   C. Kingly arrogancy violates restrictions.
      1. Multiplied horse power.
      2. Temptation to bypass Deity.
   D. No lack for man or beast.

III. Regal endowments.
   A. Incomparable acumen.
   B. No peer in learning.
   C. Prolific writer.
   D. Broad subject matter.
   E. Worldwide acclaim.

CHAPTER 5

I. Bilateral exchanges.
   A. Mutual admiration.
   B. Reciprocal helpfulness.
   C. God's providence.
   D. Building plans.

II. Mutual Pact.
   A. Appropriate skills.
   B. Wages in kind.
   C. Designated responsibilities.
   D. Contract terms approved.
   E. Wisdom's outreach.

III. Work schedules.
   A. Conscripted labor force.
   B. Rotation service periods.
   C. Distributed work load.
   D. Detailed overseers.
   E. Varied craftsmen.

CHAPTER 6

I. Building program.
   A. Chronological placement.
   B. Temple construction.
   C. Architectural conformity.
   D. Practical floor plan.
   E. Prefabricated construction.
   F. Cedar paneling.
   G. Full use of materials.

II. Building aesthetics.
   A. Acceptable with God.
   B. Intricate wood carvings.
   C. Gold overlay.
   D. Imposing enlargement in oracle.
   E. Stone carvings.
   F. Seven year project.

CHAPTER 7

I. Personal building project.
   A. Magnitude in time.
   B. Magnitude in dimensions.
   C. Magnitude in operational floor plan.

II. Metalurgical skill imported.
   A. Tribal ancestry.
   B. Paternal apprenticeship.
   C. Moldings and carvings.
   D. Artificer in grandeur.

III. Appurtenances for worship.
   A. Decorative supports.
   B. Cleansing fount.
   C. Imposing mountings.
   D. Symbolic engravings.
   E. Abundant lavers.
   F. Altar aids.
   G. Totals unaccounted for.
   H. Complete dedication.

CHAPTER 8

I. Temple initiated into service.

A. National assemblage.
   B. The oracle complete.
   C. Innumerable sacrifices.
   D. Deity's cloud.
   E. Deity's glory.
II. Temple dedication.
   A. God's prerogative.
   B. Choice of dwelling.
   C. Man's deference.
   D. God's supervisions.
   E. God's selection of builder.
   F. Covenant implications.
III. Dedication prayer.
   A. Plea for inviolate covenant.
   B. God's magnitude.
   C. God's condescension.
   D. Man's frailties.
   E. Kingly intercession.
   F. Repentant realities.
   G. Kingly blessing.
IV. Dedicatory sacrifices.
   A. Peace offerings.
   B. Vast number of offerings.
   C. Solemn national feast.
   D. Glad response.

CHAPTER 9

I. Dedication answer.
   A. Divine acceptance.
   B. Divine requirements.
   C. Divine promises.
   D. Divine warning.
II. Dedication annulment possible.
   A. Vagrant king.
   B. Straying people.
   C. Departed glory.
   D. Vivid testimony of ruin.
III. Displeasing payoff.
   A. No commensurate with service.
   B. Continuum in regional name.
   C. Tax schedule
IV. Daughter's dowry.
   A. Gift of father king.
   B. Husband's building project.
V. Deployed work force.
   A. Canaanite bondmen.
   B. Exemption of Israel.
   C. Israelite foremen.
   D. *Camelot* building program.
   E. Developed merchant marine.
   F. Emigrant sailors.

CHAPTER 10

I. International reputation.
   A. Foreign queen *inquisition*.
   B. "Pomp and circumstance."
   C. Unpretentious display.
   D. Highest quiz test score.
   E. Skepticism answered.
   F. Sovereign blessing.
   G. Gifts in gratitude.
II. International exchange.
   A. Navy commerce.
   B. Mementoes of increase.
   C. Guest gifts not small.
   D. Open market trade.
   E. Gamut of merchandise.
III. International patronage.
   A. Wisdom as a commodity.
   B. Assumed responsibilities.
   C. Tangible assets.
   D. The precious made common.
   E. Price stability.

CHAPTER 11

I. Marital instability.
   A. Wisdom fails.
   B. Insecurity intrigues.
   C. Love or lust?

I KINGS

    D. Senility on ascendancy.
    E. Idolatry, a natural step.
    F. Errant sonship.
    G. Follower — not a leader.
II. Displeased Deity.
    A. A day of reckoning prescribed.
    B. Covenant remembrances.
    C. Diminished glory.
    D. Adversaries aroused.
    E. Dubious Egyptian reliability.
    F. Damascene sanctuary.
    G. Foreman defection.
III. Deity's design.
    A. Analogous spokesman.
    B. Subjective implications.
    C. Power of choice limited.
    D. Power of choice portentous.
    E. Promised providence.
    F. Saul-pattern in Solomon.
IV. Dynasty diminishes.
    A. A matter of record.
    B. Chronology fixed.
    C. The passing pattern.

CHAPTER 12

I. Official orientation.
    A. National assembly grounds.
    B. Call for champion.
    C. Petition for relief.
    D. Contingent loyalty.
II. Patriciate in practice.
    A. Veneration for elders.
    B. Sound advice.
    C. Youthful power grab.
    D. Youth in regality.
III. Self-separation.
    A. Retaliatory tax measure.
    B. Retaliatory tax refusal.
    C. Regality in retreat.
    D. Rebel leadership.
    E. Ahijah's prophecy fulfilled.
IV. Sanctioned separation.
    A. Plans for forced reunion.
    B. Induction complete.
    C. Divine purpose revealed.
    D. Army mustered out.
V. Regal pride.
    A. First in politics.
    B. Religion and the state.
    C. Power of exile experiences.
    D. Pattern for Israel.
    E. King appointed priesthood.
    F. Copy of Judah rites.

CHAPTER 13

I. A call for repentance.
    A. Direct mission to apostate king.
    B. Defamation prediction.
    C. A king's disbelief.
    D. A reminder of power source.
    E. A petition for restoration.
    F. A futile invitation.
    G. A circumscribed mission.
II. Starved fellowship.
    A. Stirred by newscast.
    B. Outreach of kindred soul.
    C. Invitation for fellowship.
    D. Restrictions reiterated.
    E. Removal in falsehood.
    F. No safety in false belief.
    G. A Judas confession.
III. Proof of truth.
    A. Resumed journey interrupted.
    B. Unnatural natural phenomenon.

C. Late newscast.
D. A borrowed grave.
E. Sepulcher to share.
F. Worthy remembrance.
G. Accepted prophecy.
IV. Refractory regality.
A. Continued apostasy.
B. Inappropriate priesthood.
C. Sin in continuum.
D. Embryo of finality.

CHAPTER 14

I. A king's limitations.
A. Reminder in similarity in son's name.
B. Petticoat courier.
C. Subterfuge for success.
D. Spiritual sight sufficient.
II. The reason for rejection.
A. Disregard for divine directives.
B. Reciprocal retribution.
C. Dynasty terminus.
D. Derogatory simile.
E. Animal bait prospect.
F. Mission miasma.
G. Prognosticated captivity.
H. Fulfilled prediction.
J. A king's demise.
III. Parallel happenings.
A. Canaanitish maternal background.
B. Devious devotions.
C. Idolatry over-shadow.
D. National defense depleted.
E. National treasure loot.
F. Inferior replacements.
G. Lifelong fraternal enmity.
H. A change of kings.

CHAPTER 15

I. Like son — like father (cf. II Chron. 10-12).
A. Power of example.
B. Spared by Davidic covenant.
C. Continued enmity.
II. Reverted pattern.
A. Recreant to ancestoral idolatry.
B. Queen demotion for grandmother.
C. Limited reforms.
D. Sincere dedication.
III. Ancestoral groove.
A. Antagonistic to Israel.
B. Boughten protection.
C. Appropriated building material.
D. Physical debility.
IV. Contemporary vagaries.
A. Israel's old rut.
B. Intrigue and usurpation.
C. Complete dynasty change.
D. Still in the sin road.

CHAPTER 16

I. Another chance.
A. Prophetic warning.
B. Review of providence.
C. Like punishment for like evil.
D. Crown prince reigns.
II. Army coup d'etat.
A. Chariot captain conspirator.
B. Booze as an ally.
C. Retaliation possibility prevented.
D. Duo-monarchy.
E. Rebel removal.
III. Reunited Israel.
A. Building program.
B. New capital city.

I KINGS

- C. Lowest scale in evil to date.
- D. Chronological succession.
- IV. A son in same pattern.
  - A. Deeper in degradation.
  - B. Queen led to greater idolatry.
  - C. Border line building lesson.

CHAPTER 17

- I. Ahab's test.
  - A. Weather control.
  - B. Prophet's temporary provision.
  - C. Progression in providence.
  - D. Material limitations.
  - E. First things first.
  - F. Miracle life.

CHAPTER 18

- II. Ahab's threats.
  - A. Prophet prepared for confrontation.
  - B. Organized reconnaissance.
  - C. Obadiah's compassion.
  - D. Obadiah's meeting.
  - E. Obadiah's fear.
  - F. Obadiah's mission enlarged.
  - G. Obadiah's assurance.
  - H. Obadiah's report.
- III. Ahab's choice.
  - A. National assembly at Carmel.
  - B. Proof for Deity.
  - C. Elijah's plan.
    1. Proof with Deity.
    2. Magnanimity in priority.
  - D. Elijah's patience.
  - E. Elijah's sarcasm.
  - F. Elijah's preparation.
    1. Worship hour.
    2. Altar repair.
    3. Allay's accusations of secret fire.
    4. Complete confidence.
  - G. Elijah's prayer in worship.
    1. Proof of prophet.
    2. Proof of power.
  - H. Elijah's safeguard for worship.
  - I. Elijah's faith.
    1. Advice to Ahab.
    2. Prayer for rain.
    3. Belief in small signs.

CHAPTER 19

- I. Dutiful report.
  - A. The queen hears.
  - B. The queen reacts.
  - C. The queen threatens.
- II. A prophet on the run.
  - A. Fear propulsion.
  - B. Journey's end?
  - C. Abandoned hope.
  - D. Defeat after victory?
- III. A prophet prepared.
  - A. Rest and revitatlization.
  - B. A return to Horeb.
  - C. Natural protection.
  - D. The voice of introspection.
  - E. Self-vindication.
  - F. The test phenomena.
    1. Wind power.
    2. Earthquake power.
    3. Fire power.
    4. Voice power.
  - G. Iterated alibi.
- IV. A Prophet recommissioned.
  - A. Political missions.
  - B. Replacement mission.
  - C. The old and the new meet.

CHAPTER 20

I. Warmongering.
   A. Alliance for aggression.
   B. A tyrant's share.
   C. A peace keeping answer.
   D. A tyrant's unreasonableness.

II. Council of war.
   A. Review of demands and concessions.
   B. Popular support for resistance.
   C. Exchange brags.
   D. Reliance on liquid courage.
   E. Help that counts.
   F. Liquid courage sans strength.
   G. Complete victory.

III. Renewed councils.
   A. Helpful warning.
   B. Enemy alibies.
   C. Narrow vision.
   D. Renewed conflict.
   E. Iterated helpful counsel.
   F. Augmented enemy casualties.

IV. Preparations for peace.
   A. Enemy petitions.
   B. Hope in rumors.
   C. Reciprocal respect.
   D. Leniency expected and granted.
   E. Alien privileges promised.

V. The pay-off for help.
   A. Accountability revealed.
   B. Graphic analogy.
   C. Subjective application.
   D. Gloom before doom.

CHAPTER 21

I. Land hunger.
   A. King not exempt.
   B. Legitimate *surface* offer.
   C. Law limitations.
   D. Lamenting peevishness.

II. Physical hunger.
   A. Frustration.
   B. Disturbed household.
   C. Augmented greed.
   D. Transferred leadership.

III. Land grabbing.
   A. Conniving subtlety.
   B. Evil cohorts.
   C. Misused law.
   D. Gruesome report.

IV. Land possession.
   A. Squatter's rights.
   B. Judgment pronounced.
   C. Protagonist vs. antagonist.
   D. Dog food doom.

V. Postponed fulfillment.
   A. Majesty in humbleness.
   B. Mercy in control.
   C. Reckoning calendar revised.

CHAPTER 22

I. Ambition's urge.
   A. Neighbor's state visit.
   B. Recognized inactivity.
   C. Conjunctive force.
   D. Divine direction needed.

II. Divine guidance sought.
   A. Henchmen loyalty.
   B. Skeptical royalty.
      1. Final word sought.
      2. Final word doubted.
   C. Graphic proof presented.
   D. Forewarned "soloist."
   E. Circumscribed message.
   F. "Solo aria" upheld the chorus.
   G. A king's skepticism.

H. Second stanza change.
   I. A king's doubt vindicated.
   J. Divine use of evil.
III. Battle strategy.
   A. Paid prophet's arrogancy.
   B. Prophetic proof, a surety.
   C. "Unfriendly" prophet jailed.
   D. Kingly disguise for safety.
   E. Mistaken identity.
   F. A random shot.
   G. Prophetic fulfillment.
IV. Judah's ascendancy.
   A. Paternal pattern.
   B. Limited reform.
   C. Reciprocity treaties.
   D. Commercial extension.
   E. Unilateral navy control.
V. Royal primogenture.
   A. Jehoshaphat's successor.
   B. Ahab's successor.
   C. The power of example.

II KINGS

CHAPTER 1

I. Rebel strength.
   A. Death of oppressor.
   B. Health hazard.
   C. Insecure successor.
II. Wrong oracle.
   A. "Lord of the flies" insufficient.
   B. God's spokesman intercepts.
   C. The short journey.
   D. Unwelcome prediction.
   E. A man of renown.
   F. Identity established.
III. Firsthand information.
   A. Safe-conduct escourt.
   B. Proof of authenticity.
   C. Repeated endeavor.
   D. Diffidence and safety.
   E. Message unchanged.
   F. Fulfillment of prediction.
   G. Conflict in names.

CHAPTER 2

I. A prophet's promotion.
   A. Preparation announcement.
   B. Understudy's loyalty.
   C. Undergraduates' warnings.
   D. Concerned galley audience.
II. A prophet's "launching pad."
   A. Watercourse barrier eliminated.
   B. A last request.
   C. Contingent fulfillment.
   D. Spacecraft.
III. A prophet's cue.
   A. Recognition of relationship.
   B. A break with the past.
   C. Under the prophet's mantle.
IV. A prophet's status.
   A. Supported by initial act.
   B. Meets skeptical request.
   C. Reacts to needs of people.
   D. Used common agent plus faith.
   E. Above thoughtless ridicule.

F. Circuit ministry.

CHAPTER 3
I. Ahab's power for evil.
   A. Dynasty lingers.
   B. Idolatry modified by lives.
   C. Rebel regal sheepherder.
   D. Induction census.
   E. Honorable allies?
II. Jehoshaphat's sanction.
   A. Fainthearted in adversity.
   B. Divine sanction needed.
   C. Recognized spokesman.
   D. Silence without Jehoshaphat.
III. Deity's response.
   A. Physical needs provided.
   B. Promised military victory.
   C. Scorched earth policy.
   D. Enemy misinterpretation.
   E. Enemy defeat.
   F. Enemy determination.
   G. Israel's defection from battle.

CHAPTER 4
I. A creditor's backlash.
   A. Widow and orphan victims.
   B. Fraternal plea for help.
   C. Present inventory.
   D. Mutual help.
   E. Magnified faith.
   F. Multiplied resources.
II. A benefactor's backlash.
   A. Hospitality offered.
   B. Hospitality established.
   C. Hospitality rewarded.
III. A faith's backlash.
   A. Health hazard.
   B. Physical limitations.
   C. Maternal love's outreach.
   D. Recognized possible need.
   E. Firsthand help only.
   F. Above passing blame.
   G. Reciprocal response.
      1. Elisha sent.
      2. Elisha went.
      3. Elisha spent.
   H. Reward for trust.
IV. A dearth's backlash.
   A. Potluck provision.
   B. Mutual mulligan.
   C. Faulty ingredient.
   D. Right catalyst added.
   E. Forerunner of loaves and fish.

CHAPTER 5
I. Leadership limitations.
   A. Military victories common.
   B. Physical defeats alarming.
   C. Answer in forays.
   D. A child as leader in suggestion.
II. Leadership presumptions.
   A. Reciprocal message source.
   B. Wrong receiver.
   C. Wrong interpretation.
   D. Re-direction in time.
III. Leadership consternation.
   A. No fanfare.
   B. Debasing directives.
   C. Haughty resistance.
   D. Lowly logic.
IV. Leadership gratitude.
   A. Efforts to show favor.
   B. Blessing beyond price.
   C. Request replaces offer.
   D. Motives vs. actions.
V. Leadership ascendancy.
   A. Greedy Gehazi.
   B. Lying Gehazi.
   C. Shortsighted Gehazi.
   D. Suffering Gehazi.

II KINGS

CHAPTER 6
I. Building boom.
  A. Prophet's school needs.
  B. Recognized needs.
  C. Do-it-yourself program.
  D. Inspiration in personnel.
  E. Construction accident.
  F. Integrity preserved.
II. Aggressor's boom.
  A. Secret counsels valueless.
  B. Wrong answers.
  C. No quisling present.
  D. An army against one man.
III. Oppressor's doom.
  A. One-sided view.
  B. Minority replaced.
  C. Sight transference.
  D. Guide services.
  E. Prisoners of war policy.
IV. Defenders' gloom.
  A. Renewed invasion.
  B. Food scarcity as weapons.
  C. One-sided cannabalism.
  D. Misplaced blame.
  E. Recognized source.

CHAPTER 7
I. Famine end predicted.
  A. Only a miracle possibility.
  B. Skeptical acceptance.
  C. Sight experience only for doubter.
II. Right use of logic.
  A. Inevitable premise.
  B. Surprise findings.
  C. Selfish response.
  D. Self-preservation security.
  E. Report to authority.
  F. Test for possible trap.
III. Confusion in order.
  A. Spoils for takers.
  B. Price slump as foretold.
  C. Appointed director victimized.
  D. Human foibles flamboyant.

CHAPTER 8
I. Famine warning.
  A. Shunammite family's move.
  B. Seven year period.
  C. Gehazi's report on Elisha.
  D. Living proof of ministry.
  E. Complete restoration.
II. Foreign travel.
  A. Damascus visited.
  B. Royal capitulation.
  C. Regal request.
  D. Paradox in answer.
III. Foretaste in history.
  A. Countenance giveaway.
  B. Brutal picture.
  C. Commensurate disbelief.
  D. Prediction fulfillment pattern.
IV. Judah in Israel's pattern.
  A. Regal family ties.
  B. Ahab's outreach.
  C. Lost dominions.
  D. Allies against common enemy.
  E. Sick-call in order.

CHAPTER 9
I. Vicarious sanction.
  A. Less conspicuousness.
  B. Selective procedure.
  C. Special service specified.
  D. Designed demise for Baalite royalty.
  E. Secrecy demanded.
II. Immediate take-over.
  A. Unannounced confrontation.

B. Furious driving of Jehu.
   C. Messengers conscripted.
   D. Firsthand information.
   E. Treason recognized.
   F. Chickens roost at home.
III. Ahab's final pay-off.
   A. Craven sonship.
   B. Blatant banter.
   C. A queen's failure.
   D. Delayed respect thwarted.
   E. Verified prophecy.

CHAPTER 10

I. A reprisal chance.
   A. Ample reasons.
   B. Sufficient resources.
   C. The better part of valor.
II. A proof for allegiance.
   A. Destruction of claimants.
   B. Proof presented.
   C. The blameworthy.
   D. A reminder of God's truth.
   E. Ahab's blight in Judah.
III. Baal zeal in subterfuge.
   A. National worship called.
   B. Strict religious segregation.
   C. Convenient conclave.
   D. Delegated responsibility.
   E. Idol materials destroyed.
IV. Partial revival.
   A. Sparked by Ahab's stigma.
   B. Jeroboam's calves abide.
   C. Israel's "Whittling" in process.

CHAPTER 11

I. A father's daughter.
   A. Hasty usurpation.
   B. God's preservation.
   C. Safe concealment.
   D. Time element.
II. Regal restoration.
   A. Ample preparation.
   B. Careful safeguards.
   C. Strategic deployment.
   D. Strict directions.
   E. Official pronouncement.
   F. Trite response.
   G. Usurpation's termination.
III. Covenant renewal.
   A. Spiritual leadership.
   B. Political implications.
   C. National acceptance.

CHAPTER 12

I. Right regality.
   A. Royal background.
   B. Religious instruction.
   C. Reform restrictions.
II. Repair program.
   A. Designated funds.
   B. Delegated authority.
   C. Dilatory performance.
   D. Diligence delayed.
   E. Director reform.
III. Repair progress.
   A. Changed tax plan.
   B. Functioning accounting department.
   C. Workmen compensation.
   D. Priests' patrimony preserved.
IV. Reactionary foreign policy.
   A. Renewed antagonism.
   B. Rear guard action.
   C. Reward for retreat.
   D. Rebel reaction.

CHAPTER 13

I. Jeroboam's long shadow.
   A. Calf worship abounds.
   B. Judgment begins.
   C. Lost status in dominion.
II. Shadow dims.

II KINGS

    A. Prayer in humble sincerity.
    B. Compassionate response.
    C. Lessened oppression.
    D. Continued idolatry.
    E. Limited regal glory.
III. Shadow remains.
    A. King change of little consequence.
    B. Sought glory in warfare.
    C. Sick visit to Elisha.
    D. Echo of Elijah's passing.
    E. Elisha's last ministry.
    F. Object lesson limited.
    G. Success limited.
IV. Elisha's shadow.
    A. Power after death.
    B. Power to restore life.
    C. Happenstance fruitful.
V. Abraham's shadow.
    A. Israel protected by covenant.
    B. Judgment in force.
    C. Postponed rejection.
    D. Elisha's object lesson complete.

CHAPTER 14

I. Contrast continued.
    A. Judah mostly right.
    B. Israel mostly wrong.
    C. Recompense to plotters in Judah.
    D. Conspirators unpunished in Israel.
    E. Judah law conscious.
    F. Israel in compromise.
II. Over ambitious Judah.
    A. Victory over Edom.
    B. Instigated war with Israel.
    C. Thistle allegory.
    D. Lesson missed.
    E. Defeated by Israel.
    F. Victor's spoils.
    G. Victor passes first.
    H. Victim of conspirators.
III. Compassion for Israel.
    A. Jeroboam II in same shadow.
    B. Israel's glory strengthened.
    C. Divine approval because of covenant.
    D. Territory reclaimed.
    E. Favored by posterity.

CHAPTER 15

I. Limited right.
    A. No farther than predecessor.
    B. Populace unrestrained.
    C. Health quarantine.
    D. Rule by proxy.
II. Absent right.
    A. Israel's new king in the rut.
    B. Conspiracy climate.
    C. Jehu's shadow ended.
    D. Short reign.
    E. Brutality common.
    F. Under tribute.
    G. Oppressive taxes.
    H. Conspiracy's harvest.
III. Usurped right.
    A. Aggressor's victim.
    B. Israel's domain diminished.
    C. Conspiracy's sprout.
IV. Judah's right.
    A. Still limited.
    B. Kingdom's day in late afternoon.
    C. Lost glory foreshadowed.

CHAPTER 16

I. Israel overshadowed Judah.
    A. Judah's king.

- B. Human sacrifice.
- C. Widespread idolatry.
- D. Object of Syrian aggression.
II. Judah foreshadowed by Assyria.
- A. Boughten protection for Judah.
- B. Allied meeting at Damascus.
- C. Idol altar pattern.
- D. King-priest combination.
- E. Misappropriated temple altar.
- F. Misappropriated hallowed things.

CHAPTER 17

I. Assyria overshadowed Israel.
- A. Under tribute.
- B. Under governmental supervision.
- C. Under discovered duplicity.
- D. Sin's payday arrived.
II. Review of apostasy.
- A. Heathen patterns.
- B. Disobedience to God.
- C. Ample warning prophets.
- D. Stubborn rejection of right.
- E. Complete heathen practices.
- F. Easily misled.
III. Assyria replacement.
- A. In domain.
- B. In exile.
- C. In replaced populace.
- D. In revamped religion.

CHAPTER 18

I. Judah given a respite.
- A. Hezekiah's reforms.
- B. High places removed.
- C. Removed idols and groves.
- D. Serpent of brass destroyed.
- E. Divine sanction renewed.
- F. Strengthened foreign policy.
- G. Example of Israel as warning.
II. Judah facing danger.
- A. Acknowledged offense.
- B. Bribery's limitation.
- C. Nothing sacred spared.
- D. Increased pressure.
- E. Denunciation fully understood.
- F. Narrow heathen boasts.
- G. Hollow promises.
- H. False superiority.
- I. Gloomy report.

CHAPTER 19

I. A king's concern.
- A. A problem for prayer.
- B. A petition to the prophet.
- C. A promise of protection.
II. A king's warning.
- A. Dominance only delayed.
- B. No insolence.
- C. Preview of peril.
III. A king's recourse.
- A. A letter for liaison.
- B. A power problem.
- C. Appraisal of aspects.
IV. A king's assurance.
- A. God's record above repeal.
- B. Recognized arrogance.
- C. Defiance by Deity.
V. A king's battleless victory.

II KINGS

- A. Assyrian manpower loss.
- B. Assyrian withdrawal.
- C. Assyrian parricide.

CHAPTER 20

- I. A king's illness.
    - A. Mortality concern.
    - B. Divine directives.
    - C. Deity's calendar.
- II. A king's subjective prayer.
    - A. Record review.
    - B. No visible faults.
    - C. Added tears.
- III. A king's *reward?*
    - A. Life extension.
    - B. Time manipulation proof.
    - C. Common remedy cure.
- IV. A king's selfish display.
    - A. Foreign visitors.
    - B. Sick call presents.
    - C. Guided tour.
- V. A king's reprimand.
    - A. Report of tour outreach.
    - B. Twofold mission recognized.
    - C. Dire prophecy.
    - D. Present peace prospects.

CHAPTER 21

- I. A long night.
    - A. Over a half-century of evil.
    - B. Restored idolatry.
    - C. Violated temple.
    - D. Human sacrifice.
    - E. Blessings contingent on obedience.
    - F. Out-reach heathen predecessors.
- II. Pending judgment.
    - A. Covenant broken by Judah.
    - B. Ear-tingling forecast.
    - C. Israel's judgment in order.
    - D. Judgment replacement for grace.
- III. Gloom and doom.
    - A. Long night lengthened.
    - B. Conspiracy pattern.
    - C. Public judgment.
    - D. Morning twilight visible.

CHAPTER 22

- I. Free from father's faults.
    - A. Reverse direction.
    - B. Reforms begun.
    - C. Revival underway.
    - D. Reckoning unrequired.
- II. Disturbing discovery.
    - A. Doom for evil.
    - B. Diligent ears.
    - C. Determined hearts.
    - D. Demands for interpretation.
    - E. Danger delayed.
- III. Judah's judgment.
    - A. Prophecy of truth.
    - B. Point of no return reached.
    - C. Postponed execution date.

CHAPTER 23

- I. Reform zeal.
    - A. Renewal of covenant.
    - B. Subjective acceptance.
    - C. People's response.
    - D. Iconoclastic program.
    - E. Complete withdrawal from idols.
        1. Displaced idol priests.
        2. Removed worship materials.
        3. Ash heap for residue.
        4. Jeroboam's last shadow.

F. Respect for integrity.
II. Passover paramount.
   A. Regal orders.
   B. Unequaled in memory.
   C. Unmatched in national histories.
III. Political reform.
   A. Rival ideologies silenced.
   B. Deep personal commitment.
   C. Judah's night only postponed.
   D. King's integrity recognized.
   E. Rash confrontation with Pharaoh.
   F. War casualty.
   G. Inferior successor.
IV. Patterns for downfall.
   A. Egyptian intervention.
   B. Puppet of Pharaoh.
   C. Replaced underlings.
   D. Name changing pattern.

CHAPTER 24

I. Change of masters.
   A. Babylon replaced Egypt.
   B. Recalcitrant vassalage.
   C. Victim of forays.
   D. Unpardonable actions.
II. Change in name only.
   A. A new king but old ways.
   B. Egyptian limitations.
   C. Babylonian inroads.
   D. Protection by bribery tactics.
   E. Captivity installment.
   F. Vassalage change.
   G. Nature unchanged in renaming.
   H. Rebel pattern prevails.

CHAPTER 25

I. Judah's evening twilight.
   A. Besieged by Babylon.
   B. Famine as enemy weapon.
   C. Crumbled city defenses.
   D. Futile fugitive.
II. Judah's night settled.
   A. Royal captives.
   B. Cruel last visual experience.
   C. Signs of conquering force.
   D. Captivity widespread.
   E. Remnant populace occupied.
   F. The victor's spoils.
   G. The power of life and death.
   H. Vassalage personnel change.
III. Midnight nightmares.
   A. Cousin's fight renewed.
   B. Old pattern of Egyptian safety.
   C. A bright spot in captivity.

I CHRONICLES

(The first nine chapters are geneological listings in the main and offer little material for extended outline treatment. The remaining chapters of First and Second Chronicles will furnish material not found in II Samuel and I and II Kings.)

I CHRONICLES

CHAPTER 10 (cf. I Samuel 34).
I. Saul, son of Kish in eclipse.
   A. Loser in battle.
   B. Loser in authority.
   C. Loser in life.
   D. Loser with God (cf. vv. 13-14).
II. Saul in indignity.
   A. Cruel conquerors.
   B. Gloating victors.
   C. Brash arrogancy.
III. Saul in lasting respect.
   A. Decent burial.
   B. Fitting mourning period.

CHAPTER 11
I. A call to service.
   A. Divine appointment recognized.
   B. National approval.
   C. Mutual contract.
   D. Capital city conquest.
II. Outgoing service.
   A. City expansion.
   B. Personnel valor.
   C. Leadership by abilities.
   D. Loyalty responses.
   E. Inspiring self-denial.
III. Service records.

CHAPTER 12
I. Changed loyalties.
   A. Lost glory.
   B. Growing favor.
   C. Ambidextrous leaders.
II. Mustering strength.
   A. Place of assembly.
   B. Tribal census.
   C. Tested affinities.
   D. Pledged support.
   E. No territorial limitations.
III. Convivial sanction.
   A. Ceremonial festivities.
   B. Shared provisions.
   C. Joy in fellowship.

CHAPTER 13 (cf. II Sam. 6)
I. The call for religious unity.
   A. The object of unity.
   B. The depletion of the past.
   C. Complete unity.
II. The need for religious instruction.
   A. Unauthorized transportation.
   B. Unsanctified touch.
   C. Unsettling consequences.
III. The force of religious experience.
   A. Emphasized fear of God.
   B. Enlarged consternation.
   C. Endorsement in God's presence.

CHAPTER 14
I. Kingdom acceptance.
   A. Honor from Tyre.
   B. Honor by craftsmen.
   C. Honor in family.
II. Kingdom power.
   A. Tested by national enemies.
   B. Guided by prayer.
   C. Proved by valor.
III. Kingdom outreach.
   A. Stubborn opposition.
   B. Strategy in preparation.
   C. Security in multiple victories.

CHAPTER 15
I. Capital building.
   A. Royal housing.
   B. Worship facilities.

- C. National participation.
- II. Capital learning.
    - A. Lore value.
    - B. Organization by former plans.
    - C. Reasons for former failure.
    - D. Proper delegation.
- III. Capital worship.
    - A. Worship in music.
    - B. Worship in leadership.
    - C. Worship in offerings.
    - D. Worship in actions.

CHAPTER 16 (cf. Ps. 105:1-15.
Also *PSALMS IN OUTLINE*, pp. 53-54.

- I. Specifics in worship.
    - A. Place and symbol.
    - B. Appropriate sacrifices.
    - C. Full participation.
    - D. Appointed ministries.
- II. A Psalm in Worship.
    - A. The call for thanksgiving.
    - B. The urge for testimony.
    - C. The songs of praise.
    - D. The gladness in heart.
    - E. The Living in His presence.
    - F. The remembrance of blessings.
    - G. The subjective awareness.
    - H. The everlasting covenant.
    - I. The ever-present providence.
    - J. The over-shadowing protection.
    - K. The greatness of God.
    - L. The sincerity of adoration.
- III. Organization in Worship.
    - A. Choral groups.
    - B. Custodial groups (vv. 38, 43).
    - C. Altar service groups.
    - D. Orchestral groups.
- IV. The benediction.

CHAPTER 17

- I. An out reach of providence.
    - A. National blessings.
    - B. Domestic blessings.
    - C. Reciprocal blessings.
- II. Divine prerogatives.
    - A. First choice with God.
    - B. Content to dwell in tents.
    - C. Abiding presence.
    - D. Choice of leadership.
    - E. Cognizant of people's needs.
    - F. Posterity in prosperity.
    - G. Future abiding place.
- III. A man's response.
    - A. Real humility.
    - B. Recognized projection.
    - C. Regard for providence.
    - D. Revelation appraised.
    - E. Reverence in ascendency.
    - F. Redemption possibilities.

CHAPTER 18

- I. Israel's expansion.
    - A. Victories over heathenism.
    - B. Secured dominion.
    - C. Outreach of reports.
- II. Dedicated treasures.
    - A. Legitimate spoils.
    - B. Temple materials.
    - C. Personal services.
    - D. Delegated administration.

CHAPTER 19

- I. Reciprocity in neighborliness.
    - A. Kindness answering kindness.

I CHRONICLES

    B. Subtle self-judgment in control.
    C. Reciprocity backfires.
    D. Embarrassment backlashes.
II. Force in support of brashness.
    A. Mercenaries for support.
    B. Power in action.
    C. Cooperative defense.
    D. Duo-brashness in defeat.
III. Futile face-saving.
    A. Reinforcements positioned.
    B. Defenses augmented.
    C. Defenders vindicated.
    D. Offenders in duo-subjection.

CHAPTER 20

I. Recalcitrant Ammon.
    A. Aggressions of Joab.
    B. Appropriated spoils.
    C. Transferred diadem.
    D. Ancient cruelties.
II. Giant subduers.
    A. Philistine trust.
    B. Size, but no matching might.
    C. Abnormality no aid.
    D. Descendants of Jesse as victors.

CHAPTER 21

I. Evil at work.
    A. Kingish pride.
    B. Magic in numbers.
    C. Deafness to logic.
    D. Insubordination.
    E. Divine displeasure.
II. Retributive justice.
    A. Depletion measures.
    B. Remorse for egoism.
    C. Accepted blame.
    D. Faith in divine chastisement.
    E. Prescribed worship action.
III. Reverential responsibility (cf. II Sam. 24:18).
    A. Fief response.
    B. Personal obligation.
    C. Awesome reverence.

CHAPTER 22

I. Building preparation.
    A. Selected site.
    B. Labor force.
    C. Labor divisions.
    D. Material acquisition.
II. Building projection.
    A. Architectural responsibility.
    B. Personnel limitations.
    C. Divine approval.
    D. A father's blessing.
III. Building prospects.
    A. Abundant sanction.
    B. Abundant material.
    C. Abundant workmen.
    D. Abundant dedication.

CHAPTER 23

I. Coronation preparation.
    A. Authority projection.
    B. Roster of responsibility.
    C. Assigned duties.
II. Coronation background.
    A. Abrahamic covenant valid.
    B. Change of work status.
    C. Dedicated service responsibility.

CHAPTER 24

    D. Census record proration.

BIBLE HISTORY IN OUTLINE

   E. Divisions by families.
   F. Age groupings.

CHAPTER 25
   G. Worship activities.
      1. Orchestration organization.
      2. Choir organization.
      3. Organized for teaching.

CHAPTER 26-27
   H. Custodial service.
      1. Task divisions.
      2. Time divisions.
      3. Place divisions.
   I. Accounting responsibilities.
   J. Administrative assignments.

CHAPTER 28
III. Coronation fulfillment.
   A. National assembly.
   B. Regal introductory speech.
   C. Summarized recall.
   D. Logical explanation.
   E. Divine sanction contingency.
   F. Wisdom by experience.

   G. Divine blueprint.
      1. Building needs.
      2. Kingdom success.
      3. Vicarious experience.

CHAPTER 29
   H. Assembly admonitions.
      1. Recognized inexperience.
      2. Adequate material stockpile.
      3. Reckoned stewardship.
      4. Rewarding gifts.
   I. A king's blessing.
      1. God supreme in majesty.
      2. God supreme in providence.
      3. God supreme in choice.
      4. God supreme in guidance.
   J. Congregational blessing.
      1. Reverence in worship.
      2. Magnitude in offerings.
      3. Joy in fellowship.
   K. New head crowned.
   L. A king's passing.
   M. Records speak.

II CHRONICLES

CHAPTER 1
I. Auspicious beginning.
   A. Inauguration speech.
   B. Inaugural worship.
   C. Inaugural vision.
      1. Dream in the night.
      2. Urged to ask.
      3. Limitless prospect.
II. Auspicious request.
   A. Subjective.
   B. Objective.
III. Auspicious answer.

II CHRONICLES

    A. Five fold possibility.
    B. Magnanimous choice.
    C. Fivefold fulfillment.
IV. Auspicious acquisitions.
    A. Retinue.
    B. Riches.
    C. Regality.

CHAPTER 2

I. Building determination.
    A. Mind-set.
    B. Twofold project.
    C. Import contract offers.
        1. Labor skills.
        2. Abundant materials.
        3. Bilateral agreements.
II. Building approval.
    A. Worthy purpose.
    B. Providence appraised.
    C. Acceptable terms.
III. Building organization.
    A. Labor pool.
    B. Conquest agreements in action.
    C. Organized for production.

CHAPTER 3

IV. Building schedule.
    A. On selected site.
    B. On chronological record.
    C. On dimensional symmetry.
V. Building magnificance.
    A. Material excellence.
    B. Elegance in achievement.
    C. Decorative arts.
    D. Majestic sanctuary.

CHAPTER 4

I. The altar of sacrifice.
    A. Lasting material.
    B. Adequate in scope.
II. Consecration facilities.
    A. Capacity adequate.
    B. Amply supported.
        1. Worker symbols.
        2. Burden bearers.
III. Symbolic image.
    A. Directional outreach.
    B. Complete cleansing.
    C. Departure from dirt.

CHAPTER 5

I. Placement of dedicated things.
    A. Paternal respect.
    B. Placed according to use.
II. Ark processional.
    A. Tribal leadership involved.
    B. National annual assembly of men.
    C. Designated carriers used.
    D. Transfer of tabernacle articles.
III. Sacrifice in magnitude.
    A. Innumerable animal sacrifices.
    B. National scope.
IV. Ark positioned.
    A. Dedicated site.
    B. Symbols of Divine presence.
    C. Indications of permanency.
    D. Original contents.
V. Divine approval.
    A. Reverent withdrawal.
    B. Music in worship.
        1. Instruments.
        2. Voice.
    C. Enshrouded in glory.

CHAPTER 6

I. Prayer introduction.
    A. Worshipful recall.
    B. Dwelling in faith.

C. Man's contribution.
   D. God's choice.
II. Fulfillment of promises.
   A. First recipient.
   B. Past performance.
      1. Theocratic background.
      2. Tabernacle centered.
   C. Choice in action.
      1. Capital City.
      2. Dynasty in Davidic line.
III. Paternal pattern.
   A. Heart purpose.
   B. Divine restrictions.
      1. Commendation.
      2. Postponement.
   C. Scion dedicated action.
IV. Dedicatory prayer (cf. I Kings 8).
   A. Commensurate position.
      1. Before altar.
      2. Prepared podium.
   B. Humble attitude.
      1. In kneeling posture.
      2. Uplifted hands.
      3. Upward look.
   C. Recognized providence.
      1. Uniqueness.
      2. Prior provisions.
   D. Manifold petition.
      1. Continuity in fulfillment.
      2. Need for fidelity.
      3. Word magnified.
      4. God's condescension.
      5. Man's inability.
      6. Petition for hearing prayer.
      7. Request for protective vigilance.
      8. Attentive forgiveness.
      9. Equity in judgments.
      10. Protection against aggressors.
      11. Return after captivity.
      12. Release from drouth.
      13. Teaching how to walk.
      14. Isolation from natural enemies.
      15. Individual prayer attention.
      16. Strangers included.
      17. Witness outreach.
      18. Warfare protection.
      19. Remembrance for anointed.
      20. Abiding covenant.

CHAPTER 7

I. Temple dedication complete.
   A. The *amen* of Solomon's prayer.
   B. Accepted by fire.
   C. Temple shekinah.
   D. Worshiping people.
      1. Humility.
      2. Recognition of Providence.
   E. National scope sacrifices.
      1. Regal leadership.
      2. No exemptions.
   F. Installation of priests.
   G. Established mode.
   H. Expedient variation.
   I. Timed schedule.
   J. Benediction.
II. The Lord's answer.
   A. Personal application to Solomon.
   B. In recognizable precedence.
   C. God's acceptance of temple.
   D. Real prayer interests.

II CHRONICLES

    E. Contingent approach.
       1. Proper named relationship.
       2. Genuine humility.
       3. Sincere petitions.
       4. Desirous of God's presence.
       5. Real repentance.
    F. Assured results.
       1. Attentive ears.
       2. Forgiveness in reality.
       3. Healed hurts.
    G. Continued attention.
    H. Divine leadership for obedient.
    I. Divine judgment for disobedience.
    J. Punishment as true witness.

CHAPTER 8

I. Building program termination.
    A. Temple.
    B. Palace.
    C. Restored cities.
    D. City expansions.
II. Organized manpower.
    A. Canaanite labor force.
    B. Israelite leadership.
III. The queen's palace.
    A. Especially built for her.
    B. Paternal honor reserved.
IV. King's pattern in offerings.
    A. Obedience to Mosaic covenant.
       1. In time sequence.
       2. In magnitude.
    B. On appointed altar.
V. Organized for national worship.
    A. Priestly order fixed.
    B. Temple service order set.
    C. Complete compliance.
VI. Regal recreation.
    A. Seaside resort.
    B. Business and pleasure.
    C. Imports schedule.

CHAPTER 9

I. Foreign outreach.
    A. Sheba's queen.
    B. Curious cynic.
    C. Regal entourage.
    D. Oral examination.
    E. Seeing is believing.
    F. Exchange in courtesies.
II. Importation magnitude.
    A. Commerce by land and sea.
    B. Precious metals common.
    C. Violations of king's limitations.
       1. Horse "herds."
       2. Steps to altar.
       3. Pride in regality.
       4. Pride in position in commerce.
    D. Multiple recorders.
       1. Kingdom records.
       2. Life's records.

CHAPTER 10

(cf. I Kings 12:1-19).

I. A new king.
    A. Coronation rites.
    B. Referendum leadership.
    C. Legitimate request.
    D. Superficial sagacity.
       1. Face-saving conference.
       2. Congenial council.
II. Age-old conflict.
    A. Youth vs. age.
    B. Wisdom vs. brashness.
    C. Authority vs. freedoms.

       III. A king's decision.
            A. Youth speaks.
            B. Rebellion sprouts.
            C. Greed precipitates.
            D. Rebellion blooms.

CHAPTER 11

  I. Futile war efforts.
     A. Wounded ego.
     B. Vast preparation.
     C. Minus divine approval.
 II. Substitute activities.
     A. Building program.
     B. Defensive armament provisions.
     C. Response in religion.
     D. Temple worship drawing power.
     E. Family expansion.
     F. Crown prince from rebel background.

CHAPTER 12

  I. Self-exaltation.
     A. Misplaced confidence.
     B. Misplaced devotion.
     C. Displaced national prestige.
 II. Self-examination.
     A. Prophet inspired.
     B. Providence withdrawal.
     C. Precipitous foreign domination.
III. Self-humility.
     A. Assumed guilt.
     B. Foreign controls.
     C. Lost treasures.
     D. Inferior replacements.
     E. Sin's repayment.

CHAPTER 13

  I. Fraternal conflict.

     A. National pride.
     B. Inequality in numbers.
     C. The bombardment with words.
        1. Historic recall.
        2. Israel apostasy.
        3. Futile resistance.
        4. Flaunted religiosity.
        5. Judah's fidelity.
        6. Religious plea.
 II. Fraternal subtlety.
     A. Ambuscade.
     B. Prayer for help.
     C. Trumpet charge call.
     D. Shout of encouragement.
     E. Divine deliverance.
III. Fraternal victory.
     A. Dependence of God.
     B. Advantageous pursuit.
     C. Complete conquest.
     D. Augmented pride.

CHAPTER 14

  I. Regal revival.
     A. King led.
     B. Idolatry replaced.
     C. Royal decree.
 II. Peacetime developments.
     A. Urban expansion.
     B. Built for the future.
     C. God's protection acknowledged.
     D. Protective armament.
III. African invasion.
     A. Prayer defense.
     B. Supreme Divine power.
     C. Discomfited enemy.
     D. Punishing retaliation.
     E. Legal spoils of war.

CHAPTER 15

  I. Divine recognition.

II CHRONICLES

    A. Prophetic spokesman.
    B. Realistic record of events.
    C. Contrast of ideal and actuality.
    D. Admonishment for commitment.
II. National recognition.
    A. The outreach of true testimony.
    B. Self-repatriations.
    C. Drawing power of Deity.
III. National worship in practice.
    A. Renewed covenant.
    B. Self-eradicating vow.
    C. Worship in stewardship.
    D. Family reform.
    E. Seed for apostasy remain.
    F. Extended peace.

CHAPTER 16

I. Fraternal rivalry.
    A. Border fortifications.
    B. Jealous motives.
    C. Purchased protection.
    D. The pay off.
    E. Razing and raising.
II. Fraternal rebuke.
    A. Scolding seer.
    B. Shortsighted shift.
    C. Loyalty's loss.
    D. Recovered recall.
    E. Retaliatory remorse.
    F. Oppressive operations.
III. Fragrant funeral.
    A. Disease and demise.
    B. Reigning record.
    C. Pyrotechnical preparations.

CHAPTER 17

I. A worthy son.
    A. Followed paternal pattern.
    B. Filial loyalty.
    C. Faithful in worship.
    D. Fulfilled covenant.
II. The worthy project.
    A. Wise use of personnel.
    B. Widespread teaching program.
    C. Witnessing outreach.
    D. Wisdom's rewards.
III. A worthy record.
    A. Deployed storehouses.
    B. Designated leadership.
    C. Developed manpower.
    D. Delegated protection.

CHAPTER 18

I. Over-sized fraternity.
    A. Strong national ties.
    B. Fellowship for favor.
    C. Blundering brotherhood.
II. Sane scrutiny.
    A. Sacred sanction sought.
    B. Servile spokesmen.
    C. Prudent palaver.
    D. Visual pseudovindication.
III. Promised proclamation.
    A. Dependent on Deity.
    B. Seeming similarity.
    C. Prodding conscience.
    D. Deceptive design.
    E. Muscles instead of spirit.
        1. Frustrated pseudoprophet.
        2. Punished prophet.
IV. Willful warfare.
    A. Safeguarding strategy.
    B. Push for wrong potentate.
    C. Providential protection.
    D. Demise as declared.

CHAPTER 19

I. Birds of a feather???
    A. Aid in presence only???

B. Wrong witnessing.
C. Punitive pronouncement.
D. Innate inhibitors.
II. Redeeming reforms.
A. Regal repentance pattern.
B. Judges on good behavior.
C. Judgments in equity.
D. Delegated authority.

CHAPTER 20

I. Cousins as aggressors.
A. Calamity howlers.
B. Family jealousies.
C. Positioned advantages.
II. National prayer meeting.
A. The place of prayer.
B. The persons at prayer.
C. The petitions in prayer.
 1. Deity's honor.
 2. Deity's past providence.
 3. Deity's covenant.
 4. Deity's opportunity.
III. Deity's directives.
A. Faith, not fear.
B. Battle personnel.
C. Judah's battle stance.
D. Judah's victory prediction.
IV. Judah's jubilation.
A. Dedication in worship.
B. Devotion in praise.
C. Royal admonition.
D. Paeans of praise.
E. Obedient response.
V. Battle logistics.
A. Enemy against enemy.
B. Depleted invading force.
C. Abundant spoils of war.
D. Victory songs.
E. Outreaching testimony.
VI. Epitome of loyal reign.
A. Chronological record.

B. Religious record.
C. Circumscribed commerce.

CHAPTER 21

I. A king's dowry.
A. Throne to crown prince.
B. Wealth to other sons.
C. Toll of fearful jealousy.
II. A king's downfall.
A. Wrong pattern of life.
B. Revolt of conquered lands.
C. Rampant idolatry.
III. A king's denouncement.
A. Wrong inclination.
B. Willful example.
C. Widespread punishment.
D. Wearisome disease.
E. Wrested domain in reverse.
IV. A king's decease.
A. Demolished glory.
B. Devastating illness.
C. Demoted in burial.

CHAPTER 22

I. The broad way down.
A. Royal lineage intact.
B. Royal intermarriage.
C. Royal road to idolatry.
II. The broad way in bloodiness.
A. Bloodiness in war.
B. Bloodiness in sick call.
C. Bloodiness in retribution.
III. The broad way in jealous greed.
A. Dynasty designs.
B. Destruction to demurrers.
C. Derailed devastation.

CHAPTER 23

I. Revival of royalty.
A. Recalled military leadership.

II CHRONICLES

  B. Reassigned responsbilities.
  C. Restricted traffic.
  D. Rewarding response.
II. Royalty rejected.
  A. Alerted queen mother.
  B. Aroused queen.
  C. Anathematized queen.
  D. Annihilated queen.
III. Royalty in dedication.
  A. Removed signs of idolatry.
  B. Restored priestly offices.
  C. Regal procession.
  D. Reconstituted royalty on throne.

CHAPTER 24

I. Religious revival of continuum.
  A. Dedicated worship.
  B. Established family life.
  C. Temple restoration plan.
  D. Financial drive for repair costs.
  E. Haste encouraged.
  F. Levitical foot-dragging.
  G. Auditing report requested.
  H. Offering chest provided.
  I. Careful reckoning.
  J. Workmen faithfully repaid.
  K. Temple worship reinstituted.
II. Religious decline.
  A. Death of spiritual leadership.
  B. Political pressure.
  C. Compromising king.
  D. National apostasy.
  E. Divine wrath clouds.
  F. Prophets of warning wronged.
  G. Short memories about providence.
  H. Enemy invasion and spoils.
  I. Conspiracy against king.
  J. Regal support depleted.
  K. Demotion in death and burial.
III. Royal record and replacement.

CHAPTER 25

I. Partial rightness.
  A. Right in succession.
  B. Right in limited revenge.
  C. Right in delegated power.
II. Partial preparedness.
  A. Mobilized for defense-aggression?
  B. Mercenaries from brethren.
  C. Limited dependence on God.
  D. Small army victory.
  E. Great spiritual defeat.
III. Paucity in humility.
  A. Arrogance over logic.
  B. Wrong counselors.
  C. Vivid analogy.
  D. Baseless pride.
  E. Divine deterrent.
IV. Punctured ego.
  A. Military defeat.
  B. Material losses.
  C. Inglorious demise.

CHAPTER 26

I. Useful Uzziah.
  A. Real revival.
  B. Rebuilding and restoration.
  C. Right conduct.
  D. Reorganization.
    1. Refurbished economy.
    2. Reapportioned manpower.
    3. Rearmament provisions.

II. Uncompromising Uzziah.
   A. Loyalty.
   B. Dedication.
   C. Deliverance.
III. Unctuous Uzziah.
   A. Inflated ego.
   B. Insistent involvement in priestly duties.
   C. Indomitable resistence.
   D. Incurably displeased.

CHAPTER 27

I. A father's footsteps.
   A. Worship.
   B. Kingly propriety.
   C. Building expansions.
II. A Son's successes.
   A. Victories in conquest.
   B. Prosperity in reparations.
   C. Sacred sanctions.
III. A regal record.
   A. King's history.
   B. King's reign.
   C. King's passing.

CHAPTER 28

I. Steps in sin.
   A. Rebel royalty.
   B. Rebel relatives.
   C. Rebel revulsion.
   D. Rebel rejection.
II. Steps in subjection.
   A. Perennial pagans.
   B. Pernicious personages.
   C. Parsimonious pressure.
   D. Protesting prophet.
   E. Protective patrimony.
   F. Patronizing plea.
   G. Plural paternal probes.
III. Steps in stubbornness.
   A. Sanctimonious salutations.
   B. Salutariless support.
   C. Salacious sacrifices.
   D. Secluded sepulcher.

CHAPTER 29

I. Renewal in right religion.
   A. Led by new king.
   B. Lapse of minimum time.
   C. Levitical offices reclaimed.
   D. Labors multiplied.
II. Reasons reign.
   A. Punishment by divine wrath.
   B. Perverse providence.
   C. Perseverance in loyalty required.
   D. Prudent compliance.
III. Report and restoration.
   A. Complete labor report.
   B. Consecration sacrifices.
   C. Commanded performance.
   D. Commandeered Levites as priests.
   E. Complete religious experience.

CHAPTER 30

I. Outreach in evangelism.
   A. Letters of invitation.
   B. Limitations in time lapse.
   C. Loving entreaty.
   D. Laughter and scorn reception.
   E. Lean response.
II. Overwhelming revival of Passover.
   A. Much people assembled.
   B. Manpower augmented.
   C. Multitude form part of Israel.
   D. Multiple prayer application.
   E. Manifold joy in worship.

II CHRONICLES

    F. Majestic sanction for extension.

CHAPTER 31

I. Combine cleansing.
    A. Worshipping Israel working together.
    B. Rebel religion icons removed.
    C. Re-established roster of service.
    D. Regal ratio of offerings.
    E. Tithers' totals.

II. Consecrated conservation.
    A. Security storehouses.
    B. Faithful stewardship.
    C. Responsibility delegation.
    D. Service schedule set.
    E. Commitment to commandments.

CHAPTER 32

I. Foreign eyes.
    A. Judah's prosperity enticement.
    B. Threatened siege.
    C. Defense measures.
        1. Changed water course.
        2. Defense walls.
        3. Armament increase.
        4. Mobilized army of defense.
        5. Morale building speech.

II. Foreign division of forces.
    A. Propaganda campaign.
    B. Arrogant blind boasting.
    C. Misplaced confidence.
    D. Oral plus written assault.

III. Foreign failure.
    A. Prayer power defense.
    B. Silent, invisible attack.
    C. Shame-filled retreat.
    D. Victim of Parricide.

IV. Foreign influence.
    A. Gifts that blind.
    B. Regal illness cured.
    C. Record ruined by pride.
    D. Increased treasures.
    E. Exploits continued.
    F. Show-off ego.
    G. Pattern for posterity's punishment.

CHAPTER 33

I. A long downgrade trip.
    A. Heathen pattern.
    B. Re-established idolatry.
    C. Human sacrifice practiced.
    D. Desecrated temple.
    E. Full-scale following.

II. Words of warning.
    A. Faithfully declared.
    B. Deaf ear response pattern.
    C. Defeat and dejection.

III. Late lamentations.
    A. Blind eyes that begin to see.
    B. Penitential praying.
    C. Restoration and revival.
    D. Right worship practices.
    E. Partial response by people.
    F. Permanent records.

IV. Ruts remain.
    A. Stubborn successor.
    B. Indigent idolatry.
    C. Cogent conspirators.
    D. Indigenous reformation.

CHAPTER 34

I. Return to right paths.
    A. Right pattern used.
    B. Rigid direction.

C. Removal of rival idols.
   D. Retributive reactions.
   E. Renovations complete.
II. Remorseful response.
   A. Discovered Deuteronomy.
   B. Reading report.
   C. Rent robes.
   D. Contrite conscience.
   E. Placating prophetess.
III. Renewed covenant.
   A. Read to populace.
   B. Royal recapitualtion for covenant.
   C. Positionized people.
   D. Perpetual pattern.

CHAPTER 35

I. Worship at its best.
   A. Worthy object of worship.
      1. Purpose.
      2. Place.
      3. Pattern.
   B. Re-established schedule.
      1. Duties.
      2. Rotations.
   C. Adequate preparation.
   D. Brotherly concern.
   E. Worship in music.
   F. Superior magnitude.
II. Wasted well-meaning.
   A. Wrong war.
   B. Arrogant ears.

   C. Lamentable loss.
   D. Records speak.

CHAPTER 36

I. Foreign intervention.
   A. Judah's king changed by Egypt.
   B. Babylon's intervention second.
   C. Treasury spoiled.
   D. Satan's kingdom third.
   E. Babylon's voice again heard.
   F. Satan's influence continued.
II. Foreign face saving.
   A. Rebel Judah king.
   B. Idolatrous people in Judah.
   C. Prophets ignored.
   D. Babylon in retaliation.
      1. Captives in deportation to Babylon.
      2. Spoils of conquest removed to Babylon.
      3. Property damage in Judah.
   E. Overdue land sabbaths at last.
   F. Commission to rebuild Temple.

EZRA

CHAPTER 1

I. Repatriated nation.
   A. God's providence recognized.
   B. God's directives obeyed.
   C. God's use for men and materials.

II. Repatriated gifts.
   A. Israel's leadership response.
   B. Temple treasures restored to Israel.
   C. Accurate accounts.

EZRA

CHAPTER 2
I. Census count.
   A. Tribal records proof.
   B. Israel's leaders in charge.
   C. No birth "certificates" blockage.
II. Recordless exclusions.
   A. Priesthood deletions.
   B. Restricted reinstatement.
   C. Limited participation.
III. National entity.
   A. Israelite totals.
   B. Regular labor roster.
   C. Material census.
   D. Stewardship activated.
   E. Citizenship recognized.

CHAPTER 3
I. Worship calendar.
   A. The reinstitution.
   B. First things first.
   C. Mixed motivations.
   D. Daily practice.
   E. Stated set feasts.
   F. Willing worship.
II. Building brochure.
   A. Money and materials.
   B. Ruler's requirements.
   C. Building beginnings.
   D. Firm foundation.
   E. Paeans of praise.
   F. Mixed emotions.

CHAPTER 4
I. Adamant adversaries.
   A. Compromise worship plea.
   B. Limited knowledge.
   C. Personal responsibilities.
   D. Request displaced by resistance.
   E. Mercenaries at work.
II. Letter exchange.
   A. No language barrier.
   B. Selfish alibi.
   C. One-sided report.
   D. Unfavorable prediction.
   E. Supporting reply.
III. Limited research.
   A. Checks only complaints.
   B. Limited application.
   C. Selfish interpretation.
   D. Obedience spurred by desire.
   E. Force stifled project.

CHAPTER 5
I. Building progress.
   A. Prophetic proclamation.
   B. Prophetic inspiration into action.
   C. Prophetic backing.
II. Building hindrances.
   A. Questioned authority.
   B. Questioned delegation.
   C. Questioned sanctions.
   D. Requesting inquiry.
III. Building Projection.
   A. Building signs.
   B. Building purpose.
   C. Building replacement.
   D. Building time schedule.

CHAPTER 6
I. Harvest of research.
   A. Unbiased search of records.
   B. Adequate provision.
   C. Current endorsement.
   D. Royal decrees augmented.
II. Harvest of dedication.
   A. Obedience and obeisance.
   B. A finished building.
   C. Temple worhip in action.
   D. Prepared priests.

E. Participating people.
   F. Prayer and blessings for the king.

CHAPTER 7
   I. Leadership selection.
      A. Right background.
      B. Ready to serve.
      C. Reliable skills.
      D. Response of people.
   II. Leadership commission.
      A. King's decree.
      B. King's declaration.
      C. King's delegation.
   III. Leadership responsibilities.
      A. Prayer for government.
      B. Purveyor of treasures.
      C. Purchasing orders.
      D. Personal tax exemptions.
      E. Programed government.
   IV. Leadership gratitude.
      A. Thanksgiving for authority.
      B. Thankfulness for sanctuary beauty.
      C. Thankful for commission.
      D. Thankful for strength to serve.

CHAPTER 8
   I. Leadership roster.
      A. Family ties.
      B. Sons of their fathers.
      C. Assemblage review.
      D. Missing personnel.
      E. "Drafted" Levites.
   VI. Leadership commitment.
      A. Prayer and fasting.
      B. Required protection.
         1. Ashamed to accept soldiers.
         2. Resolved to use faith.
   C. Safekeeping valuable gifts.
   D. Safe journey, a reality.
   E. Delivery accomplished.
   F. Worship leadership.

CHAPTER 9
VII. Leadership accountability.
   A. Compromise in marital unions.
   B. Mismarriages led by princes and priests.
   C. Consternation and grief.
VIII. Leadership vicariously repentant.
   A. Sackcloth and ashes pattern.
   B. Sincere prayer for forgiveness.
      1. Review of sins of the past.
      2. Recalled reasons for punishment.
      3. Repetition of evils.
      4. Remorse and fear.
      5. Remembered mercy.
   C. Reliance upon divine leading.

CHAPTER 10
IX. Leadership in repentance.
   A. Offenders' confessions.
   B. Compliance with divine decree.
   C. Renewed covenant.
   D. Binding proclamation.
   E. Penalty for failures.
   F. Compliance time request.
   G. Recorded actions.
   H. Tragedy of sin.

NEHEMIAH

CHAPTER 1

I. Disquieting report from homeland.
   A. Royal job loyalty.
   B. Fraternal messengers.
   C. Unhappy people in unhappy place.
II. Disturbed servant in a strange land.
   A. Tears of vicarious remorse.
   B. Mourning period.
   C. Religiously fasting.
   D. Prayer of entreaty.
      1. Confessed sins.
      2. Kind remembrances sought.
      3. Covenant terms as binding.
      4. Favor with king requested.

CHAPTER 2

I. Heart pictures.
   A. More than nostalgia.
   B. Dutiful but disturbed.
   C. Regal psychiatry at work.
   D. Diagnosis and prescription.
II. Heart hunger.
   A. Regal sanction requested.
   B. Regal concessions granted.
   C. Divine approval assured.
III. Heart hindrances.
   A. Heathen neighbor opposition.
   B. National lethargy.
   C. Magnitude of task.
IV. Heart encouragements.
   A. Leadership council approval.
   B. Faith's harvest.
   C. Will to work revived.

CHAPTER 3

I. Building responsibilities.
   A. No exemptions of priesthood.
   B. Labor pool outreach.
   C. Prophetic families involvement.
   D. No artisan exclusions.
   E. Policital leadership as builders.
   F. Sectional delegations.
   G. Job conveniences utilized.
   H. Foreman obligations.

CHAPTER 4

II. Building bottlenecks.
   A. Jealous opposition.
   B. Satire and sarcasm.
   C. Exaggerated propaganda.
III. Building prayer interests.
   A. Petitioned strength against restraints.
   B. Retalitory wish in kind.
   C. Will to work predominant.
IV. Building stoppage threats.
   A. Enemy anger mounting.
   B. Watchful praying.
   C. Rigorous labor.
   D. "Grapevine" spies.
   E. National, family, personal incentives.
   F. Surprise element lost to foes.

G. Divided muscle power.
H. Intercom system established.
I. Daylight hours made labor day.
J. Impounded sentry duties.
K. Leadership in perseverance.

CHAPTER 5

I. Selfish servitude.
  A. The cry of the oppressed.
  B. Widespread application.
  C. Curtailed capacity to help self.
II. Self-examination.
  A. Leadership first.
  B. No exemptions for nobility.
  C. Peer judgment applied.
  D. A right example offered.
  E. Corrective restorations.
  F. Helpful compliance.
  G. Welfare covenant accepted.
  H. Graphic visual lesson.
III. Selfless public service.
  A. Unused Governor's salary.
  B. Divine inspiration.
  C. Work example pattern.
  D. Self support in practice.
  E. Prayer motivation.

CHAPTER 6

I. Subtleties instead of threats.
  A. Guise of fellowship.
  B. Subterfuge recognized.
  C. Without excuse.
  D. Persistence without "harvest."
II. Missives instead of emissaries.
  A. Catalog of accusations.
  B. Propaganda leverage.
  C. Categorical denials.
  D. Acknowledge power of threats.
III. Espionage campaign.
  A. Suggested refuge.
  B. Fear generated by compli-
  C. Faith in ascendency.
  D. Prayer power available.
IV. Victory in completion.
  A. Enviable building record.
  B. Chagrin in thwarted purpose.
  C. Family correspondence feature.
  D. Dual purpose message exchange.

CHAPTER 7

I. Security tactics.
  A. Appointed gatekeepers.
  B. Personal integrity.
  C. Definite time schedule.
  D. Detailed sentry duty.
  E. Depleted dwellings and dwellers.
II. Current census.
  A. God's purpose.
  B. Record values.
    1. Former full registery.
    2. Returnees recorded.
    3. Family genealogies.
    4. Professional rosters.
    5. Religious leaders.
    6. Polluted priest candidates.
    7. Servant listing.
    8. Livestock assessments.
  C. Monetary gifts.
    1. Family heads as pattern-setters.
    2. Priesthood follow-up.

NEHEMIAH

      3. Laity response.
  D. Settlement time schedule.

CHAPTER 8

I. Revival of learning.
  A. Inspired by the people.
  B. Citywide expectancy.
  C. Requested reading session.
  D. Reading and interpreting personnel.
  E. Reverence in Divine presence.
    1. Representatives.
    2. Written word.
II. Revival in worship.
  A. Attitudes in worship.
  B. Diffidence in His presence.
  C. Amens of ascent.
  D. Understanding ears.
  E. Joy for mourning.
  F. Shared blessings.
III. Revival time span.
  A. Seven day time lapse.
  B. Timely reinstitution of feast of booths.
  C. Long intermission remembered?

CHAPTER 9

I. Revival of confession.
  A. Restricted to Israel.
  B. Personal and national.
  C. Bible reading and prayer.
II. Revival of blessings.
  A. Blessing to God.
  B. Hallowed name recognition.
  C. Creator status.
  D. Abrahamic call.
  E. Abrahamic covenant.
III. Revival of recall.
  A. Egyptian judgment.
  B. Miracle providence (cf. v. 21).
    1. Red Sea crossing.
    2. Directed visible leadings.
    3. Spoken Law at Sinai.
    4. Manna and water.
  C. Stubborn rebellion.
    1. Hardened hearts.
    2. Dull ears.
    3. Straying feet.
    4. Idolatry.
  D. Continuous mercy.
  E. Instructional program.
  F. Land divisions.
  G. Posterity in abundance.
  H. Conquest achievements.
  I. Delight sans thanksgiving.
  J. Active oppositions.
  K. Leadership in rebellion.
IV. Revival in commitments.
  A. Acknowledged servitude.
  B. Land harvest for masters.
  C. Covenant renewal.

CHAPTER 10

I. National renewal.
  A. Designated tribal leaders.
  B. All knowledgeable persons agree.
  C. Strict bloodline restriction.
  D. Careful Sabbath observance.
II. Individual renewal.
  A. Equitable tax base.
  B. Personal responsibility in offerings.
  C. Placement responsibilities.

D. No exemptions or omissions.
E. Pledged perpetual loyalty.

CHAPTER 11

I. National pride.
  A. Assigned residence for security.
  B. Fraternal appreciation.
  C. Tribal representation.
  D. Delegated supervision.
II. National officialdom.
  A. Priesthood duty schedule.
  B. Priesthood helpers assignment.
  C. Outside temple labor force.
  D. Leadership in thanksgiving and prayer.
  E. Organized choirs.
  F. Remunerative service by king's word.
III. National citizenship.
  A. In tribal inheritances.
  B. National life established.

CHAPTER 12

I. Specifics in worship leaders.
  A. Levitical family lineage.
  B. Undeniable records.
  C. Relegated work assignments.
II. Building project dedication.
  A. Levitical leadership responsibility.
  B. Complete panoply of praise.
  C. Orchestration provided.
  D. Choir concerts.
  E. Full sanctification.
  F. Antiphonal praise program.
     1. Thanksgiving.
     2. Hymns of worship.
  G. Great sacrifices with rejoicing.
III. Accounting responsibility.
  A. Designated treasurers.
  B. First fruits and tithes.
  C. Levitical inheritance.
  D. Temple servers remembered.
  E. Complete stewardship.

CHAPTER 13

I. Reminders in reading.
  A. Bars to Ammon-Moab participation.
  B. Retributive restraints.
  C. Obedient ears and hands.
II. Deviate practices.
  A. Alliance supercedes law.
  B. Misappropriated space.
  C. Selfish resident.
  D. Curtailed benevolence.
  E. Mentor absent.
III. A new furlough.
  A. Righteous ire.
  B. Religious house cleaning.
  C. Right use restored.
IV. Sloven sacrilege.
  A. Neglect of Levites.
  B. Singers misused.
  C. Temple foresaken.
  D. Inviolate accusation.
V. Reaffirmed religious truth.
  A. Responsible safeguards.
  B. Faithful personnel.
  C. Seeking divine reassurance.
  D. Sabbath desecration record.

ESTHER 131

- E. Gatekeeper responsibility.
- F. Jew and Gentile guilt.
- G. Threat-flavored warning.
- H. Short memories.
- I. Levitical responsibilities.
- J. Wrong marriages.
- K. Solomon's long shadow.
- L. Flagrantly contaminated priesthood.
- M. Cleansed personnel in service.
- N. Repeated plea.

ESTHER

CHAPTER 1

- I. World dominon.
  - A. Kingdom expanse.
  - B. Pride in possessions.
  - C. Extended celebrations.
  - D. Lavish decor.
  - E. Twofold groupings.
  - F. Manhood's glory.
  - G. Battle of the sexes.
- II. Dominion threatened.
  - A. Commandments jeopardized.
  - B. Example as threat to all men.
  - C. Council action.
  - D. Separation decreed.
  - E. Law of perpetuity.
  - F. Safeguard to home sanctity.
  - G. Home authority protected.

CHAPTER 2

- I. Beauty contest.
  - A. Queen's replacement sought.
  - B. Organized preparation.
  - C. National identity unspecified.
- II. Beauty recognized.
  - A. Favoritism sans partiality.
  - B. Family background undisclosed.
  - C. Parental concern.
- III. Beauty in review.
  - A. Deliberate preparation.
  - B. Scheduled appearance.
  - C. Artifices unlimited.
  - D. One man judge decision.
- IV. Beauty accepted.
  - A. Artifices sans augmentation.
  - B. Unbiased approval.
  - C. Crowned beauty.
  - D. Coronation festivities.
- V. Beauty in service.
  - A. Family helpfulness.
  - B. Presence profitable.
  - C. Unquestioned messenger.
  - D. Verified report.
  - E. Recorded action.

CHAPTER 3

- I. Prime minister selection.
  - A. Delegated position.
  - B. Appropriate recognition.
  - C. Disobedient minority.
  - D. Honest inquiry.
- II. Prime minister's pride.
  - A. National loyalty.
  - B. Smoldering subterfuge.
  - C. Talking money.
- III. Prime minister's proclamation.
  - A. Regal sanction.
  - B. Wide publicity.

C. Ample preparation time.
D. Premature gloating.
E. Perplexed populace.

CHAPTER 4

I. The voice of anguish.
   A. Appropriate environment.
   B. Limits of activity.
   C. Widespread application.
II. The voice of concern.
   A. Sympathetic action.
      1. Relief measures.
      2. Sympathetic inquiry.
   B. Report of doom.
      1. Enemy bribe.
      2. Enemy plans for annihilation.
   C. Request for petition.
   D. Apprehensive hesitancy.
   E. National identity danger.
III. The voice of dedication.
   A. Ecumenical prayer request.
   B. Unity in self-denial.
   C. Dedicated to impending doom.

CHAPTER 5

I. Timorous temerity.
   A. Uninvited guest.
   B. Personal acceptance.
   C. Willing magnaninity.
II. Invested invitation.
   A. Hospitality.
   B. Limited guest list.
   C. Repetitious request.
III. Bumptious bungler.
   A. Conceited glorying.
   B. Braggadocio.
   C. Ointment fly.
   D. Feasible fulmination.

CHAPTER 6

I. Delayed sleep.
   A. Review of records.
   B. Reminder of delayed honor.
   C. Request for adequacy.
   D. Rank egotism.
II. Delayed favor.
   A. Request sidetracked.
   B. Rankling ire.
   C. Rush of chagrin.
   D. Ruin forecast.
III. Delayed guest.
   A. Defeatist retreat.
   B. Demanded presence.

CHAPTER 7

I. Banquet behests.
   A. Regal vows undergird.
   B. Disturbing disclosure.
   C. Fear and frustration.
   D. Discretion lost in bungling.
II. Regal misinterpretation.
   A. Snap judgment.
   B. Obeisance misplaced.
III. Regal revitalization.
   A. Helpful hint.
   B. Dire decree.
   C. Alacritous action.

CHAPTER 8

I. Projected honor.
   A. Secrets related.
   B. Promotion authorized.
   C. Enlarged jurisdiction.
II. Projected plea.
   A. Self-sacrifice.
   B. Selfless petition.
   C. Self-response.
III. Projected protection.
   A. Unalterable king's decree.

- B. Self-defense provisions.
- C. Proclamation in all provinces.
- IV. Projected praise.
  - A. Representation in government.
  - B. Status established.
  - C. Recruitment without pressure.

CHAPTER 9

- I. Fateful day in reverse.
  - A. Haman's decree inoperative.
  - B. Force against Jew's enemies.
  - C. Opposition fades.
  - D. Refused rightful spoils.
  - E. Royal concern.
- II. Extended amnesty.
  - A. One day extension in capital city.
  - B. Like father — like sons.
  - C. Increased toll of destruction.
  - D. Life as only profit.
  - E. Dual days of celebration.
- III. Proclamation for perpetual Purim.
  - A. Binding on Jews and proselytes.
  - B. Perpetual reminder in day name.
  - C. A yearly festivity.
  - D. National sharing (cf. v. 22).
  - E. Gifts of remembrances.

CHAPTER 10

- I. Kingdom tax schedule.
- II. Power and its delegation.
- III. Recorded greatness.
- IV. Pompless benevolent power.